ROSE ELLIOT'S
VEGETARIAN
FOUR SEASONS

A Cook's Calendar of Delicious Recipes

Random House
New York

ACKNOWLEDGEMENTS

Working on this book has been a particularly happy experience,
and I'd like to express my warmest thanks to everyone who has been involved.
To Robin Wood, for inviting me to write the book in the first place,
and to Polly Powell, for enthusiastically taking it up;
to Barbara Dixon for her hard work on the manuscript,
and to Caroline Hill, the art editor, and Joan Curtis, the designer,
for making it look so good. Special thanks to my wonderful editor, Isabel Moore,
and home economist Lyn Rutherford – both were a delight to work with,
as always, and contributed many ideas; to Alan Newnham
for his inspired photography and for making the photographic sessions
so enjoyable. And not forgetting those whose support,
help and understanding means so much to me: my husband, Robert,
my daughters, and my agent, Barbara Levy.

Edited by Isabel Moore
Designer: Joan Curtis
Photographers: Alan Newnham, Jacqui Hurst (pp. 8-9, 42-3, 76-7, 110-11)
Home Economist: Lyn Rutherford
Stylist: Maria Jacques
Illustrator: Claire Davies

For HarperCollins Publishers
Commissioning Editor: Polly Powell
Project Editor: Barbara Dixon
Art Editor: Caroline Hill
Library of Congress Cataloguing in Publication data is available.
ISBN 0-679-75419-9

Typset in Palatino
Color reproductions by Amilcare Pizzi, S.p.A.
Manufactured in Italy

2 4 6 8 9 7 5 3
First U.S. Edition

INTRODUCTION

As I worked on this book I realized more and more how much the seasons still affect us, even though, thanks to modern transportation and refrigeration, our cooking and eating are no longer tied to them in the way they once were. And I realized too how much the foods which are naturally available at a given time of year are in tune with the demands of that season and harmonize with our needs.

In winter, for instance, just when we feel like eating warming, substantial foods to keep out the cold, we have a wonderful range of root vegetables, designed by nature to be suitable for storing for many weeks. As spring approaches, cleansing, astringent foods like fresh green leafy vegetables come into season, preparing us for the lighter meals and greater physical activity which comes with the return of the longer, warmer days. Then juicy fruits and vegetables refresh us in the warmth of summer. In the fall the seasonal produce becomes more substantial and filling as we move toward winter once again.

I've discovered how much pleasure and satisfaction there is in using seasonal produce and how it is often associated with traditional festivals and celebrations throughout the year, making these more special and enjoyable. Carl Jung said that fully experiencing every chapter of our lives, from childhood to old age, is vital for our complete well-being. In a similar way I think the same can be said of the seasons, each of which has its particular pleasures and qualities as well as its challenges. Being attuned to each season means enjoying it to the full while at the same time accepting that, as in the whole of life, nothing is permanent. We have to enjoy what we have now, then let go, move on and enjoy the next moment.

So, there are a number of good reasons for using foods in season, and it can certainly make sense from an economic point of view. But, having said that, I would not like to think that anyone will feel they have to use this book rigidly. Do by all means enjoy out-of-season recipes if they take your fancy or you fall for something unseasonable but enticing in the supermarket – this kind of inspiration is all part of the pleasure of cooking. Happy cooking and eating.

A NOTE
ABOUT FOOD COMBINING

'Food combining' is nowadays becoming increasingly popular and I thought it would be helpful to include here some explanatory notes which, together with the food combining index on page 144, will enable readers to follow this system of eating.

Food combining is a way of eating in which only foods of certain types are eaten at the same meal. Probably the best-known system of food combining is that propounded by Dr. Howard Hay who was born in Hartstown, Pennsylvania in 1866: his system has in recent years found new popularity in many countries throughout the world thanks to the work of Doris Grant. She describes in detail the diet (or 'system' as Dr. Hay preferred to call it) and its amazing results in *Food Combining for Health*, by Doris Grant and Jean Joice, published by Inner Traditions.

The basic principle of the Hay system is that concentrated protein foods (meat, fish, cheese, eggs and other dairy produce) and concentrated starches (pasta, rice and other grains, bread and potatoes) should be eaten at separate meals. Most fruits can be eaten at protein meals, sweet ones such as bananas with starch meals, while fats and the majority of vegetables go with both groups. The reasoning is that because proteins and starches require different conditions for digestion, they are digested more effectively with less strain on the body when eaten separately. In addition, the Hay system emphasizes the importance of fresh fruit and vegetables in maintaining the healthy alkaline balance of the blood and recommends that at least one meal a day should consist only of 'alkaline-forming' foods – i.e. fresh fruit and vegetables.

Dr. Hay's theories are contested by some nutritionists and doctors, but those who follow the Hay diet say that results speak for themselves: they feel so much better, lose weight if they need to and become cured of problems ranging from indigestion to arthritis and eczema to diabetes.

There are a number of variations on the food-combining theme. One of the most recent is that put forward by Michel Montignac. In this system of eating, proteins and fats (or lipids, as Montignac calls them) have to be separated from starches, and only certain starches are allowed: whole wheat bread, whole wheat pastas, beans and lentils. Chocolate is allowed in this system as long as it has a high cocoa butter content (preferably 75%); and, again, vegetables (and also in this case strawberries, blackberries and raspberries) can be mixed with both protein/lipids and starches/carbohydrates.

I've been interested in food combining for some years and I've tried both the Hay system and the Montignac method. Although I'm not rigid about it, I find I do tend to 'food combine' automatically now (à la Hay) most of the time with excellent results. The food-combining index on page 144 will help you to look up the recipes which go together to make a protein or starch meal.

In the main index, on page 142, I've also included a 'V' symbol to show which recipes are suitable for a vegan diet – that is, a strict form of vegetarianism in which no dairy produce (butter, eggs or cheese etc.) is eaten.

Of course, if you wish, you can ignore all these classifications and enjoy any mixture of recipes at your meal.

CONTENTS

SPRING

SUMMER

──FALL──

──WINTER──

SPRING

SPRING

During spring the days get longer, the sun climbs higher in the sky each day, the sap rises and there's a feeling of new life and energy everywhere. Where I live, although spring does not officially begin until March we see the first promises in February, as the early crocuses and snowdrops push their way up through the hard earth and the early cherry delights us with its pink blossom – a resurgence of life that culminates in the celebration of Easter, with its focus on re-birth and resurrection. I love this time of year; the buds on the trees are bursting into leaf and the air is heady with blossom – so much external activity, yet underlying it there is a great stillness.

Spring is a time of transition. We are aware of this in the kitchen in the early spring as we use up the last of the stored fruits and vegetables and prepare for the arrival of the first fresh ones. The weather, too, at least where I live, is often unsettled. So spring cookery demands flexibility; a readiness to produce meals which protect us from the still-chilly winds and rainy days, or allow us to make the most of warm days with al fresco eating, picnics and lunches in the garden. And also to introduce new flavors as the substantial foods of winter give way to the lighter, fresher ones of the new season, as the precious early crops arrive.

It's interesting that many of these are quite astringent and even slightly bitter – rhubarb, for instance, and vegetables such as turnips, radishes, scallions and even tender young dandelion leaves – which

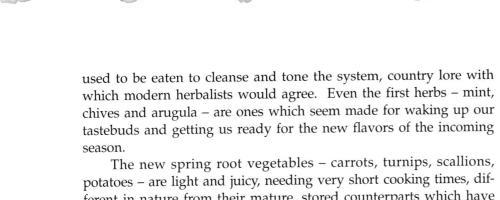

used to be eaten to cleanse and tone the system, country lore with which modern herbalists would agree. Even the first herbs – mint, chives and arugula – are ones which seem made for waking up our tastebuds and getting us ready for the new flavors of the incoming season.

The new spring root vegetables – carrots, turnips, scallions, potatoes – are light and juicy, needing very short cooking times, different in nature from their mature, stored counterparts which have nourished us so well during the cold winter months. Another early home-grown crop is fava beans, which perfectly bridge the gap between the dried pulses of winter and the light vegetables of summer. Apart from rhubarb, which although technically not a fruit is used as such, and is pleasant for a change, spring is a sparse time for fruit and one during which we can justifiably enjoy the occasional treat of exotic fruits such as pineapple, mango and kiwi.

Spring is a natural time for eggs, which can be enjoyed in a variety of sweet and savory dishes such as Frittata with Baby Carrots and Scallions (page 26), Savory Spinach Gâteau (page 27) and Hot Lemon Soufflé (page 32). From a moral point of view, although I do not wish to eat animals which have been killed, I do not object to eating eggs because in a natural environment, unless fertilized and then incubated, eggs would simply lie around until they rotted and were re-absorbed into the earth. So why not eat them? It goes without saying, though, that you should choose eggs from a reliable, salmonella-free source and eat them in moderation as part of an all-round balanced diet.

SPRING APPETIZERS

NEW VEGETABLES WITH AIOLI

You need a blender or food processor for this quick version of aioli, although you can adapt the recipe for making it by hand if you use two egg yolks instead of a whole egg, and add the oil drop by drop, as you whisk the mixture. The amount of garlic is very much a question of taste and can be reduced – or increased. The vegetables, too, can of course be varied. They can be served raw or, as in this version, cooked just to take the rawness off, then served warm. Although most people serve this as an appetizer, and a very good one it makes, my favorite way of eating this dish is as a main course, with my fingers rather than a knife and fork. It would serve four as a main course.

For a vegan version of aioli, use the special mayonnaise recipe on page 40, using soy milk instead of light cream and 2–3 garlic cloves.

FOR THE AIOLI

2-3 garlic cloves
1 egg
¼ tsp salt
¼ tsp mustard powder
2-3 grindings of black
 pepper
2 tsp wine vinegar
2 tsp lemon juice
⅞ cup light olive oil,
 vegetable oil,
 or grapeseed oil

FOR THE VEGETABLES

2 fennel
8 baby turnips
1 pound baby carrots
1 small cauliflower or
 2-4 miniature ones
1 pound baby
 zucchini

First make the aioli. Put the garlic in a food processor or blender and purée it as smoothly as you can, then add the egg, salt, mustard, pepper, vinegar and lemon juice. Blend for a minute at medium speed until the ingredients are well mixed, then turn the speed up to high and gradually add the oil, drop by drop, through the top of the goblet. When you have added about half the oil, you will hear the sound change to a 'glug-glug' noise and you can add the rest of the oil more quickly, in a thin stream. Taste the aioli and adjust the seasoning if

necessary. If it seems a bit on the thick side, you can thin it by beating in a teaspoonful or two of boiling water.

Next, prepare the vegetables. If they are young and tender, they will only need trimming and washing. Remove any tough layers from the fennel, then cut each bulb down first into quarters then into eighths. Trim and scrub the turnips and carrots. Cut the cauliflower or miniature cauliflowers as necessary, to produce chunky pieces for dipping in the aioli; halve or quarter the zucchini to make long slim batons if they are thick; if they are really slender, leave them whole.

Cook the fennel for about 8 minutes in fast-boiling water; remove the fennel, rinse under cold water to cool it quickly, then put it into a colander to drain thoroughly. Boil the turnips in the same water; as soon as they are just tender, drain and refresh them and put them in the colander with the fennel; repeat the process with the carrots and then the cauliflower. The vegetables will only take a minute or two to cook; keep testing them with the point of a knife, and remove them from the water as soon as they are just tender. Finally, cook the zucchini, which will only take about 60 seconds.

Put the aioli into a shallow bowl on a large platter. Arrange the vegetables around it, patting them dry on paper towels as necessary before serving.
SERVES 6-8

OPPOSITE: *(top) Mediterranean Cooked Green Salad, page 15, and (bottom) New Vegetables with Aioli*

JAPANESE-STYLE SALAD WITH DIPPING SAUCE AND GOMASIO

This is a light, refreshing first course. If you can't get rice vinegar, ordinary wine vinegar will do but it hasn't got quite the same sweetness and delicacy as rice vinegar (which you can get at some health stores or Chinese stores).

bunch of radishes
   (about 1 cup)
bunch of scallions
8 ounces daikon radish
   or turnip

FOR THE DIP
1 Tbs grated fresh
   ginger root

2 Tbs soy sauce
2 Tbs rice vinegar

FOR THE GOMASIO
4 Tbs sesame seeds
1 tsp salt

Wash and trim all the vegetables. Cut the radishes into lotus flowers, if you are feeling enthusiastic, and put them into a bowl of icy cold water for the petals to open. Cut the green part off each scallion to leave about 2 inches of the white part. Make cuts in the white part in from both ends toward the center, then put them into the water, too, to curl. Peel the daikon radish or turnip and cut into thin sticks; make five equal cuts down each stick almost to the base and fold in the second and fourth sections, as shown in the photograph, to make a flower. All this can be done 2 hours or so before you want to serve the salad.

While the flowers are opening, make the dip by mixing together all the ingredients and then putting it into four tiny bowls, or one larger one if you prefer. Make the gomasio by putting the sesame seeds and salt into a dry skillet set over a moderate heat. Stir for a couple of minutes or so as the sesame seeds toast and smell nutty and delicious, then remove from the heat. When the mixture has cooled, pulverize it in a coffee grinder, or with a

pestle and mortar, or in a bowl, with the end of a wooden rolling pin. Put a small quantity into four tiny bowls, or one larger one.

Drain the flowers and arrange them on four plates. If you're using tiny bowls for the dip and gomasio, you might put these on the plates, too, as part of the arrangement; or serve them separately.
SERVES 4

MEDITERRANEAN COOKED GREEN SALAD

The frequent, often daily, use of dark green leafy vegetables is one of the characteristics of the Mediterranean diet, and a typical and popular way of serving them is as a cooked salad, served warm or cold. Other ingredients, such as whole lentils or chopped hard-boiled eggs can be added, turning this simple dish into a complete light meal.

1 pound spinach or
   other dark green
   leafy vegetables
4 scallions
1 garlic clove, crushed
   (optional)

1-2 Tbs lemon juice
2-3 Tbs olive oil
salt and freshly ground
   black pepper
lemon wedges to
   garnish

Wash the spinach thoroughly. Put it into a dry saucepan, cover, and cook for 7-10 minutes, until it is tender, pressing down with a slotted spatula as it cooks. Drain the spinach in a colander, pressing out the water with the spatula. Put into a bowl.

Wash, trim and chop the scallions and add most of them to the spinach, saving some for a garnish. Mix the garlic with the lemon juice and olive oil and add to the spinach, stirring to make sure it is well distributed. Season with salt and pepper. Turn the mixture into a shallow dish and garnish with the remaining scallions and some lemon slices. Serve warm or cold, with more olive oil for people to help themselves.
SERVES 4

OPPOSITE: *Japanese-style Salad with Dipping Sauce and Gomasio*

Use a good quality soy sauce for the dipping sauce, one that's been naturally fermented, without the addition of caramel (read the label).

VEGETABLE TERRINE

This is a pretty appetizer – a loaf-shaped terrine of white farmer's cheese flecked with vegetable pieces of different colors, with a green coat of spinach and a vinaigrette sauce.

9 ounces spinach
  leaves
10 green beans
6 small scallions
½ small red bell pepper
olive oil
1 cup farmer's cheese
2 Tbs chopped fresh
  chives

2 eggs
salt and freshly ground
  black pepper

FOR THE VINAIGRETTE

2 Tbs red wine vinegar
6 Tbs olive oil

First set the oven to 325°F, then line a small loaf pan with a strip of parchment paper to cover the base and extend up the narrow ends. The deep type of loaf pan is best if you have one.

Next, half-fill a fairly large saucepan with water and bring it to a boil. Meanwhile, wash the spinach; trim and wash the beans and scallions; wash the red bell pepper and cut it into strips just less than ½ inch wide. When the water boils, put in the spinach and boil it for 1-2 minutes, until it is just soft, then drain it into a colander, saving the hot water, and refresh under cold running water. Put the hot water drained from the spinach back into the pan, bring it to a boil, and put in the beans, scallions and red bell pepper. Boil them for 2 minutes, then drain and refresh them under cold running water. (You won't need the cooking water any more, but it now makes good stock.)

Brush the loaf pan with a little olive oil, then press a thin layer of spinach on to the base and up the sides, so that they are all covered and there is enough spinach over to cover the top later. Pat the other vegetables dry on paper towels and cut them into ½-inch lengths.

Put the farmer's cheese into a bowl with the chives and beat in the eggs, then add the pieces of vegetable and some salt and pepper to taste. Spoon the mixture into the spinach-lined pan and cover the top with the rest of the spinach. Stand the pan in a roasting pan and pour boiling water round it so that it comes half-way up the sides; bake for 1 hour. Let the vegetable terrine cool completely in the pan, then chill it.

Meanwhile, make the vinaigrette by putting the vinegar and oil into a small jar with some salt and pepper and shaking until combined. When you're ready to serve the terrine, cut it into slices about ½ inch wide; put each slice on a plate and pour some vinaigrette beside it.
SERVES 6-8

YOUNG SPINACH SOUP

This soup is a great way to celebrate the coming of spring!

1 Tbs olive oil
1 onion, peeled and
  chopped
1 pound tender young
  spinach leaves

⅔ cup light cream
salt and freshly ground
  black pepper
grated nutmeg

Heat the oil in a large saucepan, put in the onion and cook gently, covered, for 10 minutes.

Meanwhile, wash and roughly chop the spinach leaves. Add them to the pan, along with 7½ cups of water. Bring to a boil, then simmer for about 15 minutes, until the spinach is very tender. Whizz to a purée in a food processor and pour back into the pan through a strainer, pushing through as much of the spinach as you can.

Stir in the cream, adjust the consistency with a little more water if necessary to make a thin, light soup, then season with salt, pepper and freshly grated nutmeg. Serve in warmed bowls.
SERVES 4

PINK GRAPEFRUIT, RUBY ORANGES AND MINT

This pretty and refreshing mixture is good as a break-fast or brunch dish as well as an appetizer.

2 pink grapefruit   4 sprigs of fresh mint
4 ruby oranges

Holding a grapefruit over a bowl to catch the juice, cut off the skin and pith with a sharp knife, like peeling an apple when you want to make a long piece of peel; cut between the transparent membranes to release the juicy sections of fruit. Repeat the process with the other grapefruit and the oranges, which are a bit more fiddly to do. Add some fresh mint leaves to the mixture, and serve.
SERVES 2-4

WATERCRESS CREAM

Make this light and refreshing appetizer just before you want to serve it, so that the color and flavor are fresh. Serve with some good bread.

bunch of watercress   salt and freshly ground
   (about 3 cups   black pepper
   trimmed watercress)
1 cup ricotta cheese

Wash the watercress, removing any tough stems or damaged leaves. Reserve 4 good sprigs for garnishing; put the rest into a food processor with the ricotta cheese and whizz to a smooth purée, or chop the watercress finely by hand then stir it into the ricotta. Either way, season with salt and freshly ground black pepper. Divide the watercress cream between four plates and garnish each with a sprig of watercress.
SERVES 4

PIQUANT CUCUMBER SALAD

This is a refreshing appetizer, given a pleasant kick by the mustard seeds.

1 cucumber   3 Tbs rice vinegar or
2 tsp white mustard   white wine vinegar
   seeds   fresh chives or young
salt and freshly ground   dill, if available
   black pepper

Peel the cucumber then cut it into quite thin slices. Layer these into a shallow dish, sprinkling the mustard seeds, some salt and a grinding of pepper between the layers. Pour the vinegar over the top. Cover the salad and leave for at least an hour, preferably longer – even overnight – for the flavors to blend. Snip over some fresh chives or dill before serving.
SERVES 4-6

KOHLRABI AND RADISH SALAD

Kohlrabi has a delicate flavor which I find pleasant, but the thing which I like about it most is its very crisp yet tender, juicy texture. It makes it perfect for early spring salads.

3 Tbs olive oil   2 kohlrabi, about
1 Tbs wine vinegar   8 ounces together
salt and freshly ground   bunch of radishes
   black pepper   (about 1 cup)

Put the oil and vinegar into a bowl with salt and pepper to taste and mix to make a simple dressing. Peel the kohlrabi quite thinly, then cut it into julienne matchsticks; wash and slice the radishes. Add the kohlrabi and radishes to the bowl and stir gently to coat everything with the dressing.
SERVES 4

If you can't get kohlrabi, use turnip.

NEW VEGETABLES AND HERBS

LITTLE FAVA BEAN AND MINT PATTIES

I like the crisp coating which chick-pea flour gives to these patties, although you could use ordinary flour, or even fry or bake them without flour, as they'll still get crisp. Some lightly seasoned yogurt is good with them, as well as a sauce made by stirring chopped chives into plain yogurt. Sliced tomatoes or a tomato salad, or Dandelion Leaf Salad, left, also go well with them.

2 pounds shelled	**salt and freshly ground**
fava beans	**black pepper**
2 Tbs chick-pea flour	**olive oil**
plus extra for coating	**lemon slices**
6-8 sprigs of fresh mint	

Cook the beans in boiling water for a few minutes until they are tender, then remove from the heat, drain, and leave until they are cool enough to handle. With your finger and thumb, pop the beans out of their grey jackets. Put the beans into a food processor with the 2 tablespoons of chick-pea flour, the mint and some salt and pepper, and whizz until a thick purée is formed. Divide this into eight portions, dip them in a little chick-pea flour and shape them into flat round patties.

Either shallow-fry the fava bean patties, turning them over so that they get crisp and brown on both sides, or bake them in the oven. To do this, set the oven to 400°F and put a cookie sheet in the oven to heat. Brush this with oil, then put the patties on it, turning them so that they are lightly coated with oil on both sides. Bake them for 12-15 minutes, turn them over and bake for about 10 minutes more to brown the other side. Serve the patties with lemon slices.
SERVES 4

LEMONY RICE WITH GREEN BEANS AND SCALLIONS

The lemon grass gives this dish a particularly good flavor but if you can't get it, some grated lemon rind does the job pretty well. The colors – primrose yellow rice and green vegetables – are very springlike. A watercress salad goes well with it, and some crunchy roasted cashewnuts or almonds, served from a small bowl so that people can help themselves. Any rice that's left over makes a good salad, served cold.

1 cup brown rice	**3-4 lemon grass**
1 tsp turmeric	**8 ounces green beans**
salt and freshly ground	**4-6 scallions**
black pepper	**2 Tbs fresh lemon juice**

Put the rice into a medium-large heavy-based saucepan, along with the turmeric, a teaspoonful of salt and 3 cups of water. Bash the lemon grass with a rolling pin to release the flavor, and add that, too, to the pan. Bring to a boil, cover and leave to cook for 35 minutes.

Meanwhile, top and tail the green beans and cut them into 1-inch lengths; trim and chop the scallions. Put these into the pan on top of the rice, without stirring, cover and cook for a further 10 minutes, or until the vegetables and rice are tender and all the liquid has been absorbed. Fish out the lemon grass and stir in the lemon juice, which will immediately brighten up the color of the rice. Stir gently to distribute everything, check the seasoning, grind in a bit of pepper, and serve.
SERVES 4

Dandelion leaves make a delightful, slightly bitter addition to a green salad. Pick a small handful of leaves in a place free from pollution, and wash them well. Add them to a base of other salad greens—I find ordinary floppy lettuce a good neutral base for this kind of salad—tearing them up as you do so and dress with vinaigrette.

OPPOSITE: *Little Fava Bean and Mint Patties*

GREEN BELL PEPPERS STUFFED WITH CAULIFLOWER CHEESE

These bell peppers make a good, easy supper dish served with a leafy salad, a tomato salad, or a cooked vegetable. Sometimes, while the bell peppers are cooking, I make a quick fresh tomato sauce (see right) to serve with them.

4 medium green bell peppers	**2 cups grated Cheddar cheese**
1 medium cauliflower	**salt and freshly ground black pepper**

Halve the bell peppers, cutting through their stems. Carefully remove the white inner part and seeds, keeping the stem intact. Put the peppers on a broiler pan, shiny-side up, and place them under a hot broiler for about 10-15 minutes, until the skin has blistered and begun to char. Remove them from the heat, cover them with a plate to keep in the steam, and leave until they're cool enough to handle.

Meanwhile, wash the cauliflower and cut it into fairly small florets. Cook these in 1 inch of boiling water, with a lid on the pan, for 4-5 minutes, or until they are just tender. Drain them immediately and put them into a bowl with half the cheese and some salt and pepper.

Slip off the blistered and charred skin from the peppers with a sharp knife – they'll come off easily – then put them back on the broiler pan. Fill each bell pepper with the cauliflower cheese mixture, dividing it between them, then sprinkle the rest of the cheese on top of them. Put the bell peppers under a hot broiler for about 10 minutes, or until the cheese is bubbling and golden brown. If serving with the tomato sauce, pour a little on each plate and place the stuffed bell pepper halves on top.
SERVES 4

OPPOSITE: *Green Bell Peppers stuffed with Cauliflower Cheese*

BRAISED SPRING VEGETABLES AND HERBS

You can use a mixture of whatever tender spring vegetables are available: new carrots, baby zucchini, baby turnips, early green beans, shallots and, nicest of all if you can get them, some of those baby artichokes about the size of large rosebuds that you can eat in their entirety. I like to serve this feast of vegetables as a main course, perhaps starting the meal with a soup, or ending with a protein-rich dessert such as Hot Lemon Soufflé (see page 32).

2½ pounds young vegetables	**salt and freshly ground black pepper**
2 Tbs olive oil	**2 Tbs chopped fresh herbs**
fresh thyme and parsley sprigs	

Prepare the vegetables, scrubbing rather than scraping them if they're really tender, and cutting them as necessary, aiming for pieces of roughly similar size. Baby artichokes, if you're using these, need any tough leaves trimming off; halve or quarter them unless they're really tiny. Quick-cooking vegetables like baby zucchini can be left whole or added toward the end of the cooking time.

Heat the oil in a large, heavy-based pan with a lid, then put in the vegetables which will take the longest: baby artichokes, followed by fennel, onions, turnips and carrots. Stir them so that they get coated with the oil, add the sprigs of thyme and parsley and salt and pepper, then pour in a scant ½ cup of water. Bring to a boil, cover and leave to cook over a gentle heat for a few minutes, until they are almost tender. Artichoke hearts may take up to 20 minutes, but the other vegetables may take as little as 4 minutes.

When they are almost tender, add quick-cooking vegetables such as zucchini, scallions, green beans, snow peas or cauliflower. Stir again, cover and cook for a few minutes longer until all the vegetables are just tender, and bathed in a very little liquid. Fish out the herbs, check the seasoning, sprinkle with the chopped fresh herbs and serve.
SERVES 2 AS A MAIN COURSE, 4 AS A SIDE DISH

To make a fresh tomato sauce, quarter 1½ pounds of tomatoes and cook them in a dry saucepan, covered, for about 15 minutes or until they're collapsed, then purée them, pass them through a strainer, and season with salt and pepper.

PASTA PRIMAVERA

A real celebration of spring and, to be honest, early summer, this is one of my favorite pasta dishes. It's well worth taking the trouble to pop the fava beans out of their skins – for the vibrant green color, apart from anything else! If you're doubtful about the whole wheat noodles in this recipe, I can only urge you to try them; I don't think you'll be disappointed.

If you don't like the idea of whole wheat noodles, use long thin pasta such as fettucine, spaghettini or vermicelli.

1 pound fava beans, about 1 cup after shelling	1 garlic clove, crushed salt and freshly ground black pepper
4 ounces snow peas	6 ounces whole wheat noodles
8 ounces asparagus	
2 Tbs butter	a few sprigs of flat-leaf parsley

Shell the beans; top and tail the snow peas; break any tough ends off the asparagus, wash it well and cut into 1-inch lengths. Cook the fava beans in fast-boiling water to cover for 2 or 3 minutes, or until the beans are tender. Strain the beans, keeping the liquid. Rinse the beans under cold water to cool them and, with your finger and thumb, pop them out of their grey skins. Re-boil the water the fava beans were cooked in and boil the snow peas for 30 seconds then drain them; re-boil the water and cook the asparagus for about 2 minutes, or until it is just tender. (This water makes excellent stock for soups.)

Melt the butter in a large pan and add the garlic; fry for a minute or two, but don't get it brown. Add all the vegetables, and some salt and pepper, cover and leave on one side while you cook the noodles. Bring a large panful of water to a boil, drop in the noodles and bring the water back to a boil. Then draw the pan off the heat, cover and leave for 4-5 minutes until the noodles are just tender but not soggy. Give them a stir and drain them.

While the noodles are cooking, re-heat the vegetables, then add them and their buttery juices to the noodles. Mix gently, season with salt and pepper, add the parsley sprigs, and serve immediately, on to warmed plates.

SERVES 2

DEEP-FRIED PARMESAN-COATED CAMEMBERT WITH SPRING BROCCOLI

The unusual thing about this recipe is the Parmesan coating, which makes it a suitable dish for food combiners (see page 5). This is usually served as an appetizer, but I love it as a main course – the lightly cooked spring broccoli goes particularly well with the gooey inside of the cheese. I don't like a sweet sauce with it myself, but if you disagree, try using some delicious apricot and peach sugar-free preserves, gently warmed in a saucepan. I've given quantities for two people here; simply double them for four.

1 × 9-ounce Camembert in individual portions	½ cup ready-grated Parmesan cheese
2 eggs, beaten	1 pound broccoli

First prepare the Camembert: dip each portion into the beaten eggs then into the ready-grated Parmesan, making sure each one is completely coated. This can be done in advance – chill the Camembert in the fridge until about 5 minutes before you want to serve the meal.

Get the broccoli ready in advance, too: remove any tough stems and break or cut the broccoli as necessary. Have ready a large saucepan with 2 inches of boiling water for cooking the broccoli, and a pan of hot deep oil for the Camembert. The fat should be 350°F or hot enough for a cube of bread to rise to the surface immediately and become golden brown in 1 minute.

Put the Camembert into the oil and let it fry for about 5 minutes, or until it is golden brown and crisp all over. At the same time, put the broccoli into the pan of water and cook, covered, for 4-5 minutes, or until just tender. Remove the Camembert from the fat with a slotted spoon and put on to two warmed plates along with the cooked broccoli. Serve immediately.

SERVES 2

OPPOSITE: *Pasta Primavera*

A VARIETY OF EGGS

SALAD MIMOSA WITH EGG

This springtime appetizer – or it could make a lovely light lunch dish – tastes as refreshing as it looks.

2 hard-boiled eggs
½ cucumber
2 Tbs wine vinegar
2 Tbs olive oil
salt
1 Tbs chopped fresh dill

1 small lettuce, an ordinary one is fine
½ bunch of watercress (about 1½ cups)
sprigs of fresh dill

Halve the eggs and remove the yolks. Finely chop the yolks and the whites, keeping them separate. Peel and thinly slice the cucumber; put it into a shallow dish and sprinkle with the vinegar, the olive oil, a little salt and 1 tablespoon of chopped dill. Wash and dry the lettuce and watercress. All this can be done in advance.

Just before you want to serve the salad, put a few lettuce leaves on four plates, tearing the larger leaves as necessary, then arrange the rest of the ingredients attractively on top. Garnish with some fresh dill sprigs.
SERVES 4

STUFFED LIGHTLY CURRIED EGGS

These make quite a filling appetizer or, served with a spring salad, a good light lunch or supper.

4 eggs, hard-boiled
2 Tbs olive oil
2 onions, peeled and finely chopped
2 tsp curry powder
½ cup finely grated Cheddar cheese

1 Tbs milk or cream
salt and freshly ground black pepper
1¼ cups plain low-fat yogurt
dash of sugar (optional)
1-2 Tbs snipped chives

Remove the shells from the eggs and keep the eggs on one side for the moment. Heat the oil in a medium pan and put in the onions; fry for 4-5 minutes, or until tender and very lightly browned, then stir in the curry powder and cook for a further minute. Remove from the heat and put half the mixture into a medium bowl.

Cut the eggs in half and scoop out the yolks without damaging the whites. Add the yolks to the onion mixture in the bowl, together with the grated cheese, milk or cream and salt and pepper to taste; mix to a thick, soft consistency. Spoon a little of this mixture into the egg whites.

Add the yogurt to the rest of the onion mixture in the bowl, mix well, then season with salt, pepper and perhaps a tiny dash of sugar. Pour a little of the yogurt sauce mixture on to four small serving dishes, put two of the stuffed eggs on each plate beside or just on top of the sauce, and sprinkle each egg with snipped chives.
SERVES 4

OPPOSITE: *(left) Savory Spinach Gâteau, page 27, and (right) Salad Mimosa with Egg*

FRITTATA WITH BABY CARROTS AND SCALLIONS

You can use any tender spring vegetables for this easy and filling dish. When they come into season, asparagus or baby artichokes are particularly good. This frittata is also very good cold – a picnic food which you can eat with your fingers.

8 ounces scallions	*4 Tbs freshly grated*
8 ounces baby carrots	*Pecorino or Parmesan*
4 eggs	*cheese*
	2 Tbs olive oil

Trim the scallions and chop them into quite small pieces; scrub the carrots and cut them as necessary – if they are very tiny, they can be left whole. Steam or boil the carrots until they are just tender; the time will vary according to how young they are, but it could be as little as 4 minutes. Don't let them get soggy. A minute or two before they're done, put in the scallions and cook them very briefly, until they, too, are just tender. Drain immediately – the water will make good stock.

Whisk the eggs and add the grated cheese. Have the broiler heating up in case you need it. Heat the oil in a large skillet and put in the drained vegetables; stir-fry them for a minute, then pour in the beaten eggs, moving the vegetables around gently to make sure the egg mixture gets right through them, and that the grated cheese is well distributed. Let the frittata cook over a moderate heat for a few minutes until the underside is cooked and lightly browned. Then, if the top is set, turn the frittata out on to a large plate and back into the skillet, so that the other side gets cooked. If the top isn't set by the time the underside is done, put the skillet under the broiler for about half a minute, then turn the frittata out and put it back into the skillet as described. Cook for a minute or two longer, until the second side is set and lightly browned, cut the frittata into wedges and serve from the skillet.
SERVES 2

The Swiss chard quiche, right, is most delicious made with cream, but for a less rich version use milk or a mixture of milk and cream.

ARUGULA SALAD

Arugula is one of those herbs which really wakes up your taste buds, and I wish it were more widely available, in good-sized bunches. Anyway, once you've procured some, wash it, tear it into pieces and put into a salad bowl with 1 tablespoon good wine vinegar, 3 tablespoons olive oil, salt and pepper, and some other salad leaves, depending on how much arugula you've been able to get. A fairly neutral leaf, like floppy lettuce, is best, providing a neutral base for the flavor of the arugula.

SWISS CHARD QUICHE

Swiss chard, with its juicy stems, tender leaves and delicate flavor, makes an excellent quiche, but if you can't get it you could substitute ordinary spinach, using both the leaves and stems.

FOR THE PASTRY	FOR THE FILLING
1 cup fine whole wheat	*8 ounces Swiss chard*
pastry flour	*2 Tbs butter*
salt	*⅞ cup cream*
5 Tbs butter	*3 egg yolks*
1 egg yolk	*salt and freshly ground*
	black pepper
	grated nutmeg

First set the oven to 400°F, then make the pastry. Sift the whole wheat flour into a bowl or food processor and add a good pinch of salt. Put in the butter and either rub it in with your fingers, or whizz in the food processor for a few seconds; add the egg yolk and a teaspoonful of water and mix to a dough. Roll this out on a lightly floured board, then slide it carefully from the board on to an 8-inch tart pan, pressing it lightly into the pan to form a shell; trim the edges. Prick the base very lightly and bake for 15 minutes, or until the pastry is crisp. Remove from the oven and turn the heat down to 325°F.

Meanwhile, make the filling. Wash the Swiss chard, separate the stalks from the leaves, and chop both. Melt the butter in a saucepan, put in the stalks, cover and cook for about 4 minutes, or until they are almost tender. Put in the leaves, cover and cook for a further 2-3 minutes, or until everything is tender. Remove from the heat and mix in the cream, add the egg yolks, salt, pepper and nutmeg to taste, stirring well. Pour the mixture into the tart shell and bake for 25-30 minutes, or until the filling is set. Serve hot, warm or cold.

SERVES 4-6

SAVORY SPINACH GATEAU

I invented this for a special meal and it brought gasps of delight when it appeared. It's not difficult to make although you do need a food processor.

FOR THE GATEAU	FOR THE FILLING
3 pounds fresh spinach or 1½ pounds frozen	*1 medium cauliflower, yielding 6 cups florets*
2 Tbs butter	*1 cup butter*
4 egg yolks	*4 egg yolks*
salt and freshly ground black pepper	*2 Tbs lemon juice*
8 egg whites	*salt*
6 Tbs ready-grated Parmesan cheese	*chervil sprigs to garnish*

Set the oven to 400°F. Line the base of three 8-inch cake pans with parchment paper, and grease the sides. If you only have two such pans, cut a circle of paper for the third, bake two of the gâteaux, then turn one out, re-line and grease the pan, and bake the third.

If you're using fresh spinach, wash it well, then put it into a large saucepan and cook over a high heat for 7-10 minutes, or until very tender. Cook frozen spinach in a little boiling water, also for

about 7 minutes. In either case, drain the spinach into a colander and press it very well to extract as much water as possible. Then put it into a food processor, along with the butter, egg yolks, salt and freshly ground black pepper, and whizz it to a smooth, creamy purée.

Whisk the egg whites until they stand in stiff peaks, then gently fold into the spinach mixture. Tip a third of the mixture into each of the pans, level the tops, then sprinkle each with 2 tablespoons of the grated Parmesan. Bake for 10 minutes, until they are golden brown on top and the centers feel firm. (If you are baking them in two batches, turn one of the gâteaux straight out, cheesy-side down, on to a large round ovenproof serving plate, re-line the pan and bake the remaining gâteau.) When all the gâteaux are done, reduce the oven setting to 325°F.

While the gâteaux are cooking, wash and trim the cauliflower, cutting it into quite small florets. Steam the cauliflower, or boil it in 1 inch of water until tender, and drain well.

Next make the sauce. Cut up the butter roughly, put it into a small saucepan and heat until it has melted and is boiling. Put the egg yolks and lemon juice into a food processor or blender with a good pinch of salt and whizz for 1 minute. With the machine running, pour the melted butter in a steady stream into the food processor or blender through the top of the goblet, and whizz for 1 minute.

Put one layer of the gâteau on an ovenproof serving plate, spread the surface with half the sauce, then put half the cauliflower on top, followed by another layer of gâteau. Cover this with sauce and cauliflower as before, then put the final layer of gâteau on top, this time with the crunchy cheese side on top. Put the gâteau, uncovered, into the oven, and leave it for 30 minutes to heat through completely before serving. Garnish with sprigs of chervil, and serve in wedges, like a cake.

SERVES 6-8

FRUITS, CUSTARDS AND CREAMS

RHUBARB CRUMBLE

This, in my experience, is one of those 'spring wouldn't be the same without' kind of desserts. Fortunately, it's also one of the easiest to make. It's good with some cream or thick yogurt.

2 pounds rhubarb	**½ cup soft butter**
¼ cup sugar	**or vegetable**
¼ tsp ground cloves	**margarine**
½ tsp ground cinnamon	**½ cup plus 1 Tbs**
	brown sugar

FOR THE CRUMBLE
1½ cups self-rising
whole wheat flour

Set the oven to 400°F.

Cut the root ends and leafy tops off the rhubarb, then cut the stalks into 1-inch lengths and put them into a shallow ovenproof dish. Sprinkle them with the sugar, ground cloves and cinnamon.

To make the crumble, sift the flour into a bowl, adding the bran from the sifter too. With your fingertips, rub the butter or vegetable margarine into the flour until the mixture resembles fine breadcrumbs. Add the sugar and rub lightly again, to form a crumbly mixture. Spoon this on top of the rhubarb in an even layer, covering it completely. Bake for about 30 minutes, or until the crumble is crisp and lightly browned and the rhubarb feels tender when tested through the crumble with the point of a knife.
SERVES 4

MANGO AND CARDAMOM PARFAIT

I love both mango and cardamom, with its eucalyptus-like flavor. Together they make an exquisite ice-cream parfait which you can freeze in a loaf pan, without stirring, and serve in slices.

1 medium ripe mango	**⅔ cup heavy cream**
6-8 cardamom pods	**slices of ripe mango**
4 egg yolks	**and chopped**
⅓ cup sugar	**pistachio nuts to**
	decorate

Peel the mango, cut the flesh into chunks and put into a food processor. Crush the cardamom and remove the pods, then crush the seeds as much as you can, preferably with a pestle and mortar. Add them to the mango, and whizz for a minute or two until you have a completely smooth purée. Pour this through a fairly coarse nylon strainer to remove any larger pieces of cardamom.

Whisk the egg yolks until they are thick. Put the sugar into a small saucepan with 2 tablespoons of water and heat gently until the sugar has dissolved. Then boil for 2-3 minutes, until the mixture reaches 225°F on a candy thermometer or a little of the syrup forms a thread when pulled between your finger and thumb. Pour this over the egg yolks, then whisk for 4-5 minutes, until the mixture is very thick and pale. Stir the mango purée into the egg yolk mixture. Whisk the cream until it is thick but not stiff, then fold this in too. Pour the mixture into a small loaf pan and freeze until solid.

Remove the parfait 15 minutes before you want to serve it. Run the blade of a knife around the edges and invert the pan over a plate, giving it a firm shake; it should come out with no problems. Decorate with mango slices and chopped pistachios.
SERVES 8

To slice a mango, cut downwards about ¼ inch from one side of the stem, then slice it the same distance the other side of the stem, thus avoiding the pit. Then remove the skin, and cut as much flesh away from the pit as you can.

OPPOSITE: *Mango and Cardamom Parfait*

SPRING FRUIT SALAD WITH VIOLETS

This fruit salad makes the most of what fruit there is during spring. It's naturally sweetened with grape juice and is most refreshing: I love to eat it for breakfast, particularly a late and leisurely Sunday one. You probably won't need all the grape juice for the fruit salad, but any that's over is nice to drink with it. (The violets are an optional extra for special occasions.)

1 honeydew melon or similar, or part of one if it's huge	1⅓ cups seedless green grapes
4-6 kiwis	1 bottle or carton of white grape juice
	small bunch of violets

Halve the melon, remove the seeds and cut the flesh into pieces; peel and slice the kiwis; remove the grapes from their stems and wash them. Put all the fruits into a bowl – they look especially good in a glass one – and pour in enough grape juice to moisten them well. Remove some violets from their stems and float them on top of the fruit salad. Serve as soon as possible.
SERVES 4

LITTLE COFFEE CREAMS

For a vegan version of little coffee creams, use either vegan yogurt (from health stores) or soft tofu, whizzed in a food processor.

I like these coffee creams best when they are made with mascarpone cheese, which is rich, smooth and very creamy. However, thick, creamy yogurt or very fresh ricotta cheese are also good. It doesn't matter whether the instant coffee is with or without caffeine as long as it's a good quality one with a robust flavor.

1 cup mascarpone, thick, creamy yogurt or ricotta cheese	2 heaped tsp sugar chocolate-covered coffee beans to decorate (optional)
2 tsp good-quality strong instant coffee	

Put the mascarpone, yogurt or ricotta cheese into a bowl and stir a little to make it smooth. Put the coffee granules into a cup and add about a tablespoonful of almost-boiling water – just enough to dissolve them. Add the coffee to the bowl, along with the sugar, and stir until it's all well-combined.

Spoon the mixture into two bowls, and chill until you're ready to serve them. Decorate with two or three chocolate coffee beans, if you have them.
SERVES 2

SPRING FRUIT COMPOTE

This delightful compôte is sweetened with apricot and peach sugar-free preserves instead of sugar. Make sure the pineapple is sweet and ripe; it should smell syrupy, a bit like canned pineapple, and one of the inner leaves should come out quite easily when you pull it. Kiwis are nicest if they give a bit when you press them. I don't think this compôte needs any accompaniments; it's good just as it is, for a dessert or as a special breakfast dish.

1 small ripe pineapple	4 kiwis
1 cup apricot and peach sugar-free preserves	2 dessert apples

Cut the leafy top off the pineapple, cut the fruit into quarters and cut the peel and inner core off each quarter. Scoop out any 'eyes' with the point of a knife, then cut the fruit into chunky pieces and put them in a bowl with the apricot and peach preserves, mixing well. Peel the kiwis and slice them into thin rounds; peel, core and slice the apples. Add these to the bowl and stir gently.

Cover and leave for at least 30 minutes, preferably 1-2 hours, for the flavors to blend.
SERVES 4

OPPOSITE: *Spring Fruit Salad with Violets*

HOT LEMON SOUFFLE WITH APRICOT COULIS

Apricot coulis freezes well, so it's useful to make extra and freeze in suitably sized containers.

This makes a good springtime dessert, hot and warming for still-chilly days but at the same time light and refreshing. The base can be prepared in advance, leaving only the whisking and folding-in of the egg whites to be done before you put it into the oven. It's good served with pouring cream and perhaps some seasonal fruits, and especially marvelous with the coulis.

2 Tbs butter plus a little for greasing	grated rind of 2 lemons
¼ cup flour	1 Tbs lemon juice
⅞ cup milk	3 egg yolks
¼ cup sugar	4 egg whites

Use the extra butter to grease a 1-quart soufflé dish. Tie a piece of parchment paper around the outside of the dish to extend by 2 inches or so, to allow the soufflé to rise above the top of the dish.

Melt the remaining butter in a medium saucepan. When it froths, stir in the flour, cook over the heat for a moment or two and add the milk, stirring until it forms a smooth paste. Add the sugar, lemon rind and juice, then leave on one side until you are ready to finish the soufflé.

Set the oven to 325°F. Gently reheat the flour mixture just to soften it, but don't get it too hot, then remove it from the heat and stir in the egg yolks. Whisk the egg whites until they stand in stiff peaks. Mix a heaping tablespoon of egg white into the flour mixture to loosen it, then fold in the rest of the egg white. Pour the mixture into the soufflé dish, gently level the top, then run your thumb or a knife round the top edge to remove the soufflé from the edges of the dish and help it to rise well. Bake the soufflé for 30-35 minutes, or until it has risen well and just wobbles a little in the center when shaken. Remove the band of paper and serve immediately, with the Apricot Coulis.
SERVES 4

APRICOT COULIS

Put 1 cup dried apricots into a saucepan, cover with plenty of water and leave to soak overnight. Next day, add 2 Tbs sugar, a vanilla bean if you have one, and more water if necessary so that the apricots are well covered. Bring to a boil, then let them simmer, uncovered, for about an hour until nearly all the water has gone and the apricots are very tender and bathed in a glossy syrup. Cool, then remove the vanilla bean (wash it and leave it to dry, to be used again). Purée the apricots thoroughly in a blender, adding a little water if the mixture is very thick. Serve in a jug, with the soufflé.

CHOCOLATE MOUSSE WITH ORANGE CREAM

Cold, velvety-smooth, rich chocolate with a topping of orange-flavored whipped cream makes an irresistible finale to any meal. It needs to be made several hours before you want to eat it – even the day before.

7 ounces bittersweet chocolate, at least 50% cocoa solids	⅔ cup heavy cream
	1 Tbs Cointreau or other orange liqueur
2 Tbs butter	sugar
5 eggs	
1 orange	

Break up the chocolate and put it into a large bowl with the butter. Stand the bowl over a saucepan of gently simmering water and leave for about 10 minutes until the chocolate has melted. Meanwhile, separate the eggs, putting the whites into a large bowl and the yolks into a small one.

Whisk the whites until they are stiff but not breaking up. Remove the bowl of chocolate from the pan and stir in the egg yolks, followed by a good tablespoonful of the egg white. Then tip in the rest of the egg white and fold it in very gently using a metal spoon, until there is no more white to be seen and the mixture is light and fluffy. Pour the mixture into six smallish individual glass dishes or ramekins and put into the fridge to set and chill for 6 hours or more.

Just before you want to serve the chocolate mousse, prepare the orange topping. First, scrub the orange in hot water, then with a zester remove several long strands of rind for decoration; grate the rest to make about ¼ teaspoonful. Whisk the cream until it holds its shape, add the grated orange rind, Cointreau and a little sugar to taste and whisk again lightly. Spoon this mixture on top of the chocolate mousse and decorate with the strands of orange rind.

SERVES 6

FLORIDA FRUIT CUP

A taste of sunshine to cheer up chilly spring days, this fruit cup is made from the tropical fruits which are good at this time of the year, and you can vary the exact composition according to what's available. The pink grapefruit makes a pleasant addition, and the passion fruit permeate the whole dish with their exotic flavor. It makes a particularly wonderful brunch offering – but it's good any time.

1 large pink grapefruit	*8 ounces lichee nuts*
2 oranges	*1 ripe mango*
⅔ cup seedless grapes	*2 passion fruit*
2 apples	

Holding the grapefruit over a bowl, cut off the peel in one long strip using a sawing action and making sure that you cut off the white pith as well as the skin. Cut the flesh away from between the white transparent membranes and, when you've removed all the flesh, squeeze out any remaining juice. Do the same thing with the oranges, then wash the grapes and add these to the bowl; wash and slice the apples, removing their skin or not according to its condition. If using fresh lichee nuts, remove first

the skin and then the shiny brown pits from them using a sharp, pointed knife. Alternatively, use canned lichees and rinse off the syrup. Add the lychees to the bowl. Cut right down the mango on both sides of the big flat pit, starting about ¼ inch each side of the stalk. Peel and slice the flesh, cutting away as much as you can from around the pit and adding that too. Finally, cut the passion fruit in half, scoop out the flesh, including the seeds, and add this. Stir gently. Cover until needed.

It's best made half an hour or so before you want to eat it, to give the flavors a chance to blend and the juices to run, making a natural syrup.

SERVES 4-6

SPRING MENUS

MENU

A DINNER
FRESH FROM THE
GARDEN FOR FOUR

Cream of Turnip Soup
Hot Herb Bread

Twice-Baked Individual Soufflés
Creamy Tomato Sauce
Platter of Fresh Vegetables

Spiced Rhubarb Compôte with
Brown Sugar Meringues

COUNTDOWN

Up to one week in advance:
Make the meringues, which can be kept in an
air-tight container.

Up to one day before:
The following dishes can be made in advance, covered
and kept in the fridge: the soup; the herb bread, prepared
ready for cooking and wrapped in foil; the Twice-Baked
Soufflés, turned out into a casserole dish ready for their
final baking; the Tomato Sauce; the Rhubarb Compôte.
If you are going to microwave the vegetable platter,
this can also be cooked, covered and kept in the fridge.

40 minutes before the meal:
Heat the oven. Put in the herb bread 20 minutes before
you want to eat; 5 minutes later put in the Soufflés.
Gently reheat the soup and sauce; just before you want to
serve the meal reheat the vegetables in the microwave or
cook them if you haven't done so already.

CREAM OF TURNIP SOUP

*If the turnips really are 'fresh from the garden', some
or all of the leafy green tops can be used in this soup
too; if not, add some watercress, to give pungency.*

**1 pound turnips, plus
  3 ounces of the leaves,
  or watercress
1 onion, peeled and
  chopped
1 Tbs butter
4 Tbs heavy cream**

**salt and freshly ground
  black pepper
grated nutmeg
extra cream and
  chopped chives to
  garnish**

Scrub the turnips and cut them into even-sized dice;
wash and roughly chop the leaves or watercress.
Melt the butter in a large saucepan and put in the
onion; cover and cook for 5 minutes, then add the
turnips and the green tops or watercress and cook,
covered, for a further 5 minutes. Pour in 3¾ cups of
water, bring to a boil and simmer for about 20 minutes, or until the vegetables are tender.

Purée the soup thoroughly in a blender, then
pour it back into the saucepan and stir in the cream,
salt, pepper and nutmeg to taste. To serve, garnish
with cream and chopped chives

OPPOSITE: *A Dinner Fresh from the Garden
for Four*

HOT HERB BREAD

You can use whatever herbs are available; a few fresh chives and a bit of thyme, if you can get it, otherwise just some dried thyme.

1 whole wheat or
   multigrain baguette
6 Tbs butter

1 Tbs chopped fresh
   chives and a sprig of
   fresh thyme, chopped,
   or ½ tsp dried thyme

Make diagonal cuts in the whole wheat or multi-grain baguette about 1 inch apart, without cutting right through the bottom crust of the bread. Beat the butter until it's soft, then mix in the chives and thyme or the dried thyme. Spread the cut surfaces of the bread with the herb butter, then wrap the bread in foil – you may need to break the loaf in half so that it will fit into the oven.

Bake the bread for 15-20 minutes in a hot oven – it will bake perfectly with the soufflés – until the butter has melted and the bread is very hot. Serve at once, with the soup.

TWICE-BAKED INDIVIDUAL SOUFFLES

This is my food-combining (see page 5) version of this modern classic, using farmer's cheese or skim milk cheese for the base instead of the usual thick sauce, to make a completely protein dish. It's very convenient, because everything can be done in advance except for the final baking of the soufflés. They can even be made and frozen in their dish, ready to be quickly defrosted and baked.

butter for greasing
8 Tbs ready-grated
   Parmesan cheese
1 cup farmer's cheese or
   skim milk cheese
4 egg yolks

1¼ cups grated Gruyère
   cheese
5 egg whites
salt and freshly ground
   black pepper

A good wine to accompany this menu would be an aromatic dry white such as Sancerre, or a medium-bodied red such as a Red Burgundy.

Set the oven to 350°F. Generously grease eight ramekins, dariole molds or old cups, then sprinkle the insides with Parmesan, using 4 tablespoons. Put the farmer's cheese or skim milk cheese into a bowl and mash it until it's smooth, then gradually mix in the egg yolks and half the grated Gruyère cheese. Whisk the egg whites with a clean, greasefree whisk until they are standing in peaks, and stir a heaped tablespoonful into the egg yolk mixture to loosen it. Fold in the rest of the egg whites gently. Spoon the mixture into the ramekins, molds or cups: it can come level with the top, but don't pile it up any higher.

Stand them in a roasting pan, pour boiling water round to come halfway up the sides and bake for 15 minutes, until they are risen and set. Remove from the oven and leave to get cold – they'll sink a bit. Loosen the edges and turn them out. (It's easiest to turn them out on to your hand, then transfer them to an ovenproof serving dish.) Sprinkle each with some of the remaining Gruyère cheese then with the rest of the Parmesan cheese.

They can now wait until you are ready to bake them. Then, heat the oven to 425°F, and bake them for 15-20 minutes, or until they are puffed up and golden brown. Serve at once.

CREAMY TOMATO SAUCE

1 Tbs olive oil
1 small onion, peeled
   and finely chopped
2 pounds tomatoes

salt and freshly ground
   black pepper
4 Tbs cream

Heat the oil in a large saucepan and add the onion; fry for 5 minutes without browning. Quarter the tomatoes and add them to the pan. Cover and cook over a gentle heat for 10-15 minutes, or until the tomatoes have collapsed, then purée in a blender, pass through a strainer, and season. Just before you want to serve the sauce, re-heat it gently and add the cream. Check the seasoning, then serve.

PLATTER OF FRESH VEGETABLES

A platter of fresh baby vegetables is one of the joys of late spring and early summer. The exact composition is up to you – and your garden or supplier – this is just a suggestion. Trim and cut the vegetables as little as possible and cook until they're just tender.

6 ounces baby carrots
6 ounces baby turnips
6 ounces baby green
  beans
6 ounces baby
  zucchini
6 ounces sugar snap
  peas

2-3 baby cauliflowers,
  depending on the size
4 Tbs butter
2 Tbs fresh lemon juice
salt and freshly ground
  black pepper
chopped fresh parsley

Wash and gently scrub the carrots and turnips, leaving some of the green leaves still attached. Wash, top and tail the green beans, baby zucchini and sugar snap peas; wash, trim and quarter the cauliflowers (or cut them as necessary, depending on the size). The easiest way to cook a variety of vegetables like this is in a steamer – or a stack of steamers – over a large saucepan of water, since you can add the vegetables in sequence according to how long they'll take. This saves having to use several saucepans. The exact timing depends on the size of the vegetables, but if they're young and tender, none of them will take more than about 4 minutes at the most. If you wish, you can cook them separately, in advance, under-cooking them slightly, then put them into a vegetable dish, cover with a plate and microwave them just before serving.

When the vegetables are cooked, quickly melt the butter in a saucepan with the lemon juice and a good seasoning of salt and pepper, then pour this over the cooked vegetables; sprinkle with some chopped parsley just before you serve them.

SPICED RHUBARB COMPOTE

This easy-to-make recipe is a particularly good way to use the new season's rhubarb, and is delicious with the crunchy Brown Sugar Meringues below.

2 pounds rhubarb
¼ cup sugar
8 cloves

good pinch of ground
  ginger

Trim the rhubarb and strip off any stringy bits then cut into 1-inch lengths and put into a heavy-based saucepan with the sugar, 4 tablespoons of water, the cloves and ginger. Cover and cook over a gentle heat for about 5 minutes, or until soft. Transfer the rhubarb to a bowl, removing the cloves as you do so, cover and chill.

Serve with the brown sugar meringues, and, if wished, some softly whipped cream.

BROWN SUGAR MERINGUES

The brown sugar in these meringues gives them a pleasant caramel-like flavor.

2 egg whites
¼ cup superfine sugar

¼ cup dark brown
  sugar

Set the oven to 150°F or to your lowest setting. Line a cookie sheet with parchment paper. Whisk the egg whites until they are very stiff. Now whisk in first the superfine sugar, then the dark brown sugar, a little at a time, whisking well to make a glossy mixture. Shape spoonfuls of the mixture on to the cookie sheet, leaving some space around them as they spread a little. Bake them for 2-3 hours, or until they are dry and crisp. Pick one up and look at the base of it to make sure that it is dry right through. Cool on the cookie sheet then store them in an airtight container.

MENU

A LATE SPRING PICNIC FOR FOUR

Light Leek Soup

Tian of Spring Vegetables with Special Mayonnaise

Salade Nicoise with New Potatoes and Scallions

Little Lemon Grass Creams

LIGHT LEEK SOUP

In my experience, unless you're very lucky with the weather a soup makes the most welcome appetizer on a late spring picnic – and on many a summer one, too. This one is made from the last of the leeks. Take it in vacuum flasks and serve it into cups or bowls, whichever are most convenient. It's helpful to have spoons, too, to get up the last dregs of the delicious mixture. If the weather does happen to be boiling hot, by the way, this soup is also good served chilled.

1½ pounds leeks	*salt and freshly ground*
1 Tbs olive oil	*black pepper*
5 cups water	*freshly grated nutmeg*
4 Tbs cream	

Trim the roots and inedible leaf parts off the leeks, then slit them up one side and rinse under cold running water, pulling them open to make sure you get them really clean. Cut in half downwards, down again, and then across thinly, resulting in quite small pieces.

Heat the olive oil in a large saucepan and put in the leeks, stir, then cover and let them cook very gently for 10 minutes, stirring a couple of times. Add the water and let the soup simmer for about 20 minutes, or until the leeks are very tender. Purée about two-thirds of the soup in a blender – leave the rest as it is to add texture. Stir in the cream and season the soup well with salt, black pepper and freshly grated nutmeg. If you want to eat it hot, pour into vacuum flasks immediately; if cold, cool first then pack into flasks.

COUNTDOWN

Up to one day before:
The soup, Tian, Special Mayonnaise and Lemon Grass Creams can be made in advance, covered securely in foil and kept in the fridge if convenient. You can also cook the potatoes, beans and hardboiled eggs for the salad, ready to assemble it on the day.

On the day:
Reheat the soup gently and put into a vacuum flask; complete the salad, put into a suitable container or bowl and cover securely with foil.

OPPOSITE: *A Late Spring Picnic for Four*

TIAN OF SPRING VEGETABLES WITH SPECIAL MAYONNAISE

A light or medium-bodied dry white wine such as Frascati, Chablis or Muscadet goes well with this menu, with plenty of still or sparkling water or fruit juice as an alternative.

I'm particularly fond of this easy, economical dish which can be made from any combination of seasonal vegetables, although I prefer it when some leafy green ones are included. The fresh herbs, too, can be varied according to what is available – I particularly like the flavor of fresh dill. It's good served either hot with some cooked vegetables and perhaps a tomato or yogurt sauce or, as suggested here, cold with mayonnaise (or a yogurt sauce) and a tomato and basil salad.

bunch of scallions	2 eggs
1 pound zucchini	2 Tbs chopped fresh
8 ounces Swiss chard	herbs
or spinach	salt and freshly ground
1 cup small cultivated	black pepper
mushrooms	⅓ cup freshly grated
2 Tbs olive oil	Parmesan cheese

Set the oven to 350°F. Wash and trim the scallions and zucchini, then slice the scallions and cut the zucchini into small dice. Wash the chard or spinach, removing the stems and chop both the stems and the leaves, keeping them separate. Rinse and halve the mushrooms.

Heat the oil in a large saucepan and put in the prepared scallions, zucchini and chard or spinach stems. Cover the pan and cook for 5 minutes, then add the chard or spinach leaves and the mushrooms and cook for a further 5 minutes, uncovered. Remove the pan from the heat and beat in the eggs, then stir in the fresh herbs and salt and pepper to taste. Spoon the vegetable mixture into one large shallow ovenproof dish or four smaller ones, spread the top level and sprinkle with the grated Parmesan cheese. Bake for about 30 minutes if you are using a large dish or 20 minutes for smaller dishes, or until set and lightly browned. Serve the tian hot or cold.

SPECIAL MAYONNAISE

You could use a good-quality bought mayonnaise jazzed up a bit with some lemon juice and freshly ground black pepper for the Tian, left, but a homemade one is nicer if you have the time to make it. I think that this is rather a special recipe because, although it looks and tastes like a perfectly straightforward mayonnaise, it does not contain egg yolk. The original idea came to me when I was experimenting with vegan mayonnaises (you can make this recipe vegan by using soy milk instead of the cream), and then I realized how useful it would be for anyone worried about salmonella. It's a bit easier to make than a normal mayonnaise, because you don't have to be quite so careful about adding the oil, but it's still best to do this quite slowly until the mayonnaise shows signs of thickening. It will keep, well-covered, for a week in the fridge.

4 Tbs light cream	⅞ cup light olive oil,
¼ tsp mustard powder	grapeseed or peanut
salt and freshly ground	oil
black pepper	1 Tbs lemon juice
	1 Tbs red wine vinegar

Put the light cream into a bowl with the mustard powder and a good seasoning of salt and pepper, and mix them together. Add the oil gradually, a drop at a time, whisking well after each addition, exactly as if you were making an egg-yolk mayonnaise. When about half the oil has been added and the mixture has emulsified, you can add the rest more quickly in a thin, steady stream, but still whisking all the time. Finally, add the lemon juice and vinegar and stir them in very gently in one direction only, which will further thicken the mixture because of the effect of the acid on the cream. Check the seasoning – this mayonnaise needs plenty of salt and pepper.

Should the mayonnaise curdle as you're making it, you can easily remedy the situation if you start again with a tablespoon of cream in a clean bowl and whisk in the curdled mixture a bit at a time. I have just done exactly this when I was testing this recipe, and it's fine!

SALADE NICOISE WITH NEW POTATOES AND SCALLIONS

*1 pound baby new
  potatoes, scrubbed
  but not peeled*
*8 ounces young green
  beans*
2 Tbs red wine vinegar
6 Tbs olive oil
*salt and freshly ground
  black pepper*

4 tomatoes
*4 hard-boiled eggs,
  peeled*
bunch of scallions
⅓-⅔ cup black olives

Cook the potatoes in enough boiling water to cover for 10-15 minutes, or until they are just tender; drain them. Top and tail the green beans as necessary and cook them in 1 inch of boiling water for 2-4 minutes, or until they, too, are just tender then drain them. Put the vinegar, oil and some salt and pepper into a large bowl, put in the potatoes and beans, turn gently so that they are all coated with the dressing, and leave to cool.

Cut the tomatoes and eggs into quarters or eighths and chop the scallions. Add these to the bowl, together with the olives, and stir in gently. Serve cold.

LITTLE LEMON GRASS CREAMS

Every year in the UK a national supermarket holds a nationwide contest to find the best young cooks between the ages of 9 and 15, and very inspiring it is. At one of the regional finals which I attended, one of the competitors, Caroline Godsmark, made some exquisite lemon grass creams, and it is from her that I got the idea for this fragrant dessert.

3 lemon grass
⅔ cup milk
⅔ cup light cream
2 eggs and 2 egg yolks

3 Tbs sugar
*herb flowers such as
  sage to decorate*

Set the oven to 325°F.

Put the lemon grass on a board and bash it with a rolling pin to crush it and release the flavor. Put the crushed lemon grass into a saucepan with the milk and cream and bring to a boil, then cover and leave for 15 minutes for the flavor to infuse.

Meanwhile, whisk the eggs and egg yolks with the sugar until frothy but not thick. Remove the lemon grass from the milk and cream and bring back to a boil, then pour them over the egg and sugar mixture. Strain this into four ramekins or custard cups and put them into a roasting pan. Cover with foil, pour boiling water around them to come two-thirds up the sides of the dishes, and bake for about 40-45 minutes until the custards are set.

Remove them from the oven, take them out of the pan and leave to cool. Decorate with herb flowers before serving.

SUMMER

SUMMER

With the sun moving daily towards its highest point above the horizon, the days become even longer and sunnier, and the evenings are now warm and light. There is a feeling of relaxation and conviviality as we spend more time outside, making contact with other people, enjoying the fresh air and the sights and sounds of summer. The summer solstice marks midsummer when the sun reaches its zenith, and for me there is something especially magical about this time of year; it is a time of celebration for all the benefits bestowed by the sun to life on earth, demonstrated by the burgeoning growth and fruiting of plants all around us.

Summer vegetables are mainly light and juicy; zucchini, tomatoes, delicate summer spinach, tender young peas, fennel, many varieties of salad leaf and, of course, home-grown asparagus, for me one of the peaks of the culinary calendar for its short season which, where I live, lasts from the end of May until midsummer's day, although imported asparagus continues to be available after that. Summer fruits, too, have a high water content, to quench thirst and refresh parched throats. Perhaps the watermelon, much-loved in hot countries, is the best example of this, but soft fruits such as strawberries and raspberries, not to mention peaches and nectarines, are also freely available, juicy and cooling. They form the basis of some delectable summer desserts and can make a light meal in themselves – in the intense heat they may be the only thing you fancy. Strawberries, in particular, still say 'summer' to me, even though I see them in my local supermarket all the year round. And edible flowers such as roses, nasturtiums, marigolds, borage, pinks and

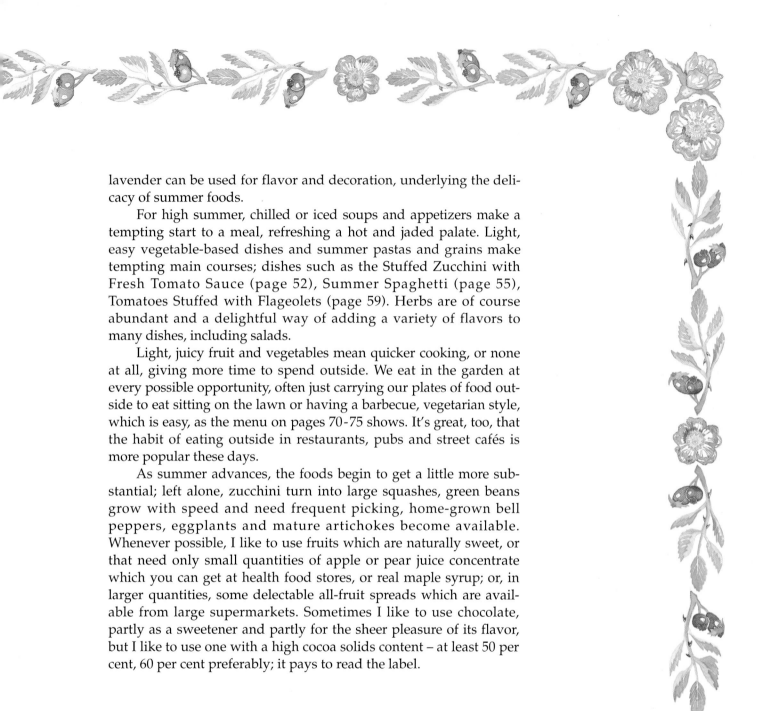

lavender can be used for flavor and decoration, underlying the delicacy of summer foods.

For high summer, chilled or iced soups and appetizers make a tempting start to a meal, refreshing a hot and jaded palate. Light, easy vegetable-based dishes and summer pastas and grains make tempting main courses; dishes such as the Stuffed Zucchini with Fresh Tomato Sauce (page 52), Summer Spaghetti (page 55), Tomatoes Stuffed with Flageolets (page 59). Herbs are of course abundant and a delightful way of adding a variety of flavors to many dishes, including salads.

Light, juicy fruit and vegetables mean quicker cooking, or none at all, giving more time to spend outside. We eat in the garden at every possible opportunity, often just carrying our plates of food outside to eat sitting on the lawn or having a barbecue, vegetarian style, which is easy, as the menu on pages 70-75 shows. It's great, too, that the habit of eating outside in restaurants, pubs and street cafés is more popular these days.

As summer advances, the foods begin to get a little more substantial; left alone, zucchini turn into large squashes, green beans grow with speed and need frequent picking, home-grown bell peppers, eggplants and mature artichokes become available. Whenever possible, I like to use fruits which are naturally sweet, or that need only small quantities of apple or pear juice concentrate which you can get at health food stores, or real maple syrup; or, in larger quantities, some delectable all-fruit spreads which are available from large supermarkets. Sometimes I like to use chocolate, partly as a sweetener and partly for the sheer pleasure of its flavor, but I like to use one with a high cocoa solids content – at least 50 per cent, 60 per cent preferably; it pays to read the label.

CHILLED SOUPS AND APPETIZERS

WATERMELON AND MINT

a good-sized piece of watermelon

8 sprigs of fresh mint

I enjoy this for its color as much as anything, although watermelon and mint together make a refreshing combination on a hot day.

Cut the skin off the watermelon and remove the seeds; cut the flesh into manageable-sized pieces and put them into a bowl. Tear the leaves from four of the mint sprigs and add to the bowl. Mix, then cover and chill until required. Spoon the mixture into four individual dishes – it looks pretty in glass ones – and decorate each with a sprig of mint.
SERVES 4

ICED LETTUCE SOUP

2 pounds outside lettuce leaves
2 Tbs olive oil
1 onion, peeled and chopped
2 or 3 sprigs of fresh mint

4 Tbs light cream
salt and freshly ground black pepper
chopped mint to garnish, and extra cream if wished

Outside leaves of lettuce which are too tough for a salad are fine for this refreshing soup.

Wash the lettuce leaves well then shred them. Heat the oil in a large saucepan and put in the onion; cover and cook for 5 minutes, add the lettuce and mint, cover again, and cook for a further 5 minutes. Pour in 3¾ cups of water, bring up to a boil and simmer for about 15 minutes, or until the vegetables are very tender.

Purée the soup thoroughly in a blender, then pour it through a strainer into a pan. Stir in the cream and season with salt and pepper. Cool, then chill the soup. Serve in bowls, garnished with some chopped mint and a swirl of cream if liked.
SERVES 4

TOMATO SORBET

This tomato sorbet makes a most refreshing appetizer on a summer's day. You do need a food processor in order to make it.

1 Tbs olive oil
1 onion, peeled and chopped
1 pound tomatoes
2 strips of lemon peel
salt and freshly ground black pepper

TO SERVE
lettuce leaves
chopped fresh chives or basil

Heat the oil in a large saucepan, add the onion, cover and cook for 5 minutes without browning. Meanwhile, chop the tomatoes roughly (there's no need to peel them) and add them to the pan, along with the lemon peel. Cover and cook gently for a further 15-20 minutes, or until the tomatoes have collapsed to a purée. Remove from the heat, purée in a blender, lemon peel and all, then pass the mixture through a strainer. Season well with salt and freshly ground black pepper. Pour into a shallow container so that the tomato purée is no more than ½ inch thick, cool and freeze.

Just before you want to serve the sorbet, put two or three tender lettuce leaves on four serving plates or glass dishes. Take the sorbet out of the fridge, turn it out on to a chopping board and, with a sharp knife, cut it into small pieces, about ½ inch square. Put these into the food processor and whizz for a minute or two, until the mixture turns to a smooth ice and holds together. Quickly put scoops of this on to the plates, on top of the lettuce. Sprinkle the chopped chives or basil over the top of the ice and serve.
SERVES 4

OPPOSITE: *(top) Tomato Sorbet and (bottom) Iced Lettuce Soup*

STUFFED ZUCCHINI BLOSSOMS

Zucchini blossoms are not easy to come by unless you grow your own, though sometimes kind friends who grow zucchini will provide them, or farm stands may give you some if you ask them. If you can get hold of them, they make a delightful light appetizer, which can be made rather more substantial by the addition of some fresh tomato sauce (see page 52) if you wish.

4 ounces mozzarella cheese (packed in water)	salt and freshly ground black pepper
8 zucchini blossoms	ready-grated Parmesan cheese
2 eggs	olive oil
	slices of lemon to serve

Cut the mozzarella cheese into eight pieces the right size to fit into the zucchini blossoms. With your fingers, pinch out the stamens from inside the blossoms, then put a piece of mozzarella cheese inside each one. Fold the tips of the petals over so that the cheese is fully enclosed.

Separate the eggs; whisk the whites until they're stiff, then beat the yolks a little to break them up, and fold in the whites. Season with salt and pepper. Holding the zucchini blossoms by the green baby zucchini part, dip the blossoms first into the egg mixture, making sure they are completely coated, then into the ready-grated Parmesan cheese. Fry them in a little olive oil, turning them over after a minute or two so that the blossoms get brown and crisp all over. (They will only take 3-4 minutes in all to cook.) Drain them on paper towels and serve immediately on warmed, individual plates. Garnish each plate with a slice of lemon.

SERVES 4

FAVA BEAN PATE WITH BROILED FENNEL

I think that this pâté is best if you take the time to pop the beans out of their skins first, although you can make it without doing this – in which case it will have a more chewy texture. If you don't want to do the fennel, some bread would also go well with it.

1 pound shelled fava beans	2 fennel bulbs olive oil
2 Tbs butter	1 Tbs red wine vinegar
2 Tbs lemon juice	black olives
salt and freshly ground black pepper	

Cook the fava beans in boiling water for a few minutes until they are done, then drain them. With your finger and thumb, pop them out of their grey skins; discard the skins. Put the beans into a food processor with the butter, lemon juice and some salt and pepper and whizz to a thick green purée. Season the mixture, put it into a bowl and cover.

Prepare the fennel by removing any tough leaves or pieces of stem, but leaving enough of the stem to hold the leaves together at the base. Cut each down first into halves, then into quarters and eighths, so that they are still joined together at the base if possible. Steam or parboil the fennel for about 8 minutes, or until it is just tender without being at all soggy. Drain well and dry with paper towels. Brush both fennel with oil and sprinkle with some salt and pepper, then broil them until they are lightly charred on both sides: this will take about 15 minutes. Cover until required. Make a simple dressing by putting the vinegar into a screwtop jar with 3 tablespoons olive oil and some salt and pepper and shaking well to mix.

To assemble the dish, spoon some of the pâté on to four individual serving plates, add some black olives, put four pieces of broiled fennel on each plate, and spoon a little dressing on top of the pâté.
SERVES 4

Served with salad, both these recipes make good light meals, in which case they will serve 2-3 people.

OPPOSITE: *Fava Bean Pâté with Broiled Fennel*

ARTICHOKES STUFFED WITH LEMON CREAM

Although these are a bit fiddly to prepare, they're so good that it's worth the effort – and as they're served cold, you can get all the main preparation done well in advance.

4 globe artichokes
1 lemon
½ cup heavy cream
1 Tbs chopped chives

salt and freshly ground
    black pepper

First, half-fill two large saucepans with water and put them on the stove to heat. Next, prepare the artichokes by cutting the bases level and removing any damaged lower leaves. For a restaurant-style presentation, you can trim the points off the leaves with kitchen scissors to make them neat; I don't always bother with this. Wash the artichokes well under cold running water, pulling back the leaves as much as you can, then divide them between the pans of boiling water.

Squeeze the juice from the lemon and reserve 2 tablespoons. Add the rest to the artichokes, dividing it between the pans. Let the artichokes simmer away for about 45 minutes, or until one of the lower leaves pulls off easily. Remove the artichokes from the water and leave them upside down in a colander to drain.

When the artichokes are cool enough to handle, gently pull back all the leaves to reveal the inner, baby leaves which cover the choke; grasp these firmly and pull them out then, with a sharp knife, cut out the remaining choke, being careful to get out all the prickly bits without taking away any more of the delicious flesh than you have to. Rinse the inside of the artichokes gently under cold water, pat them dry and leave them until just before you want to serve them.

Just before serving make the filling. Put the reserved lemon juice into a bowl and add the cream, chives, and salt and pepper. Stir the mixture gently with a spoon until it thickens to a floppy state, but don't get it too stiff. Put each artichoke on to an individual plate, pull back the leaves and spoon some of the cream mixture into the center. Serve at once. It's best to eat this dish by pulling off the outer leaves one by one and dipping their bases in the dressing, then eating the artichoke base and the remaining dressing with a knife and fork.
SERVES 4

CHILLED CUCUMBER SOUP

This is a light and refreshing soup to make at the height of summer when cucumbers are good and plentiful. If you haven't any home-made vegetable stock (which can simply be the water saved from cooking tasty vegetables such leeks or fennel), it's better to use water rather than a bouillon cube.

1 Tbs olive oil
1 onion, peeled and
    chopped
2 cucumbers
8-10 sprigs of fresh
    mint

1¼ cups vegetable stock
    or water
4-6 Tbs cream
salt and freshly ground
    black pepper
a little chopped fresh
    mint to garnish

Heat the olive oil in a large saucepan and put in the onion; cover and cook gently for 10 minutes until tender.

Meanwhile, peel and roughly dice the cucumbers. Add these to the onion, along with the sprigs of mint, cover the pan again and leave over a gentle heat for about 20 minutes, or until the cucumber is very tender and transparent. Purée the mixture in a blender, including the mint sprigs, then return it to the saucepan and stir in the stock or water and cream. Season with salt and freshly ground black pepper and leave the soup to cool, then chill it.

Check the seasoning just before you serve the soup because chilling dulls the flavor of foods, then ladle the soup into chilled bowls and sprinkle a little chopped mint on top of each.
SERVES 4

SUMMER BEAN AND FRESH HERB SALAD

The cooked beans absorb flavors well, making this a fragrant salad, refreshing yet quite satisfying. If you want to cook your own beans rather than using canned ones, you'll need 1 cup cannellini, navy or flageolet beans. Soak them in plenty of cold water for several hours, simmer them in fresh water for about 1 hour (a little more for the first two types, a little less for the flageolets) until the beans are tender, then drain. You can dress the salad while the beans are still hot. Some warm crusty bread or rolls go well with this.

3½ cups canned cannellini or flageolet beans, or a mixture of both
4 Tbs chopped fresh mixed herbs such as chives, chervil, parsley, tarragon, mint or dill

1 Tbs red wine vinegar
3 Tbs olive oil
salt and freshly ground black pepper
1 small lettuce

Drain the beans and put them into a bowl along with the fresh herbs, wine vinegar, olive oil and some salt and pepper to taste. Mix well, then cover and leave until you're ready to serve the salad. (The longer you can leave it the better, because it will give the flavors a chance to develop and blend.) Meanwhile, wash the lettuce and put the leaves into a plastic bag in the fridge to chill them and make them crisp.

To serve the salad, put one or two lettuce leaves on individual serving plates, stir the bean mixture then spoon some of it on top of the lettuce.
SERVES 4-6

EASY SUMMER TOMATO SOUP

This is a soup which really makes the most of summer tomatoes, and it couldn't be easier to make.

2 Tbs olive oil
1 onion, peeled and chopped
2¼ pounds tomatoes

salt and freshly ground black pepper
a little milk or light cream (optional)
fresh basil

Heat the oil in a large saucepan, add the onion, and cook, covered, for 5 minutes or so. Meanwhile, wash and chop the tomatoes roughly (there's no need to skin or seed them) and add them to the pan, along with a sprinkling of salt. Cover and cook gently for a further 15 minutes, or until the tomatoes have collapsed. Purée them in a blender and pour them through a strainer into the pan. Add 1¼ cups of water, or milk if you prefer, and a tablespoonful or so of light cream if you're using this.

The soup is also very good without any of these embellishments; just add some water to thin it to a nice light consistency, season with salt and freshly ground black pepper, and snip some fresh basil over the top. Chill the soup before serving – or serve it hot if you prefer.
SERVES 4

SUMMER VEGETABLES AND SALADS

SUNSHINE RATATOUILLE

4 Tbs olive oil
1 pound onions,
    peeled and chopped
1 pound red bell
    peppers, chopped
2 garlic cloves
1 pound eggplants
1½ pounds tomatoes
salt and freshly ground
    black pepper
chopped fresh parsley

*This version of
ratatouille always
works well for me,
and it is quick and
easy. It's good both
hot and cold, as a
first course – or as a
main course for a
light summer meal,
which is how I like
to serve it, with the
salad suggested here.*

Heat the oil in a large saucepan and put in the onions and red bell peppers. Cover and cook, without browning, for 10 minutes. Meanwhile, peel and crush the garlic and cut the eggplants into ½-inch dice. Add these to the pan, stir well, cover again and cook gently for a further 10 minutes.

Put the tomatoes into a large bowl, cover with boiling water and leave for 30-60 seconds, or until the skins will slip off; drain and peel. Quarter the tomatoes, then remove and discard the seeds. Chop the flesh and add to the saucepan. Give it another stir, cover and cook for a further 10 minutes, or until all the vegetables are tender. Check the seasoning, adding more salt and a grinding of pepper, and serve with some chopped parsley on top.
SERVES 2-4

GREEN SALAD WITH SHAVINGS OF PARMESAN

Put 1 tablespoon wine vinegar and 3 tablespoons olive oil into a bowl with a seasoning of salt and pepper. Give them a stir to make a quick dressing, then put some crisp salad greens on top. Some chopped fresh herbs are good too. Just before you want to serve the salad, stir the leaves gently to coat them lightly in the dressing, and add some thin slivers of Parmesan cheese.

STUFFED ZUCCHINI WITH FRESH TOMATO SAUCE

These light and summery zucchini are good served with some green beans and perhaps some buttery new potatoes.

4 plump zucchini,
    each about 4 ounces
1¼ cups Boursin cheese
    flavored with garlic
    and herbs
sprigs of fresh dill
    to garnish

FOR THE SAUCE

1 Tbs olive oil
1 small onion, peeled
    and finely chopped
2 pounds tomatoes
salt and freshly ground
    black pepper

First make the sauce. Heat the oil in a large saucepan, add the onion and fry for 5 minutes without browning. Meanwhile, quarter the tomatoes and add them to the pan. Cover and cook over a gentle heat for 10-15 minutes, or until the tomatoes have collapsed, then purée in a blender, pass through a strainer, and season. Set aside.

Halve the zucchini and cook them in 1 inch of boiling water in a saucepan until they are just tender: about 3 minutes. Drain them well. Scoop out the seeds with a pointed teaspoon or grapefruit spoon and discard them. Place the zucchini in a shallow casserole or broiler pan. Mash the cream cheese to soften it a bit, then put some into the cavity of each zucchini, dividing it between them and piling it up well. Put the zucchini under a hot broiler until they are heated through and the cheese has just started to brown.

Meanwhile, gently reheat the tomato sauce to serve with them. Garnish with the sprigs of dill just before serving.
SERVES 4

OPPOSITE: *Stuffed Zucchini with Fresh Tomato Sauce*

ASPARAGUS WITH HOLLANDAISE SAUCE

As far as I'm concerned, this is one of the best treats of summer. I like to serve lots of asparagus with this buttery sauce as a main course, accompanied by a salad such as the Bibb Lettuce, Field Lettuce and Herbs one, right. A flinty white wine and fresh strawberries would complete the meal.

1 pound asparagus	*2 egg yolks*
½ cup butter	*sea salt*
1 Tbs lemon juice	

First prepare the asparagus by removing any tough stalk ends, then shaving down the stems a bit with a vegetable parer to trim further if necessary. Wash the stems, especially the heads, well. Cook the asparagus in a steamer until it is just tender, 5-10 minutes, or in a pan of boiling water to cover: it will take a little less time. Drain well.

Meanwhile, make the sauce. Cut up the butter roughly, put it into a small saucepan and heat until it has melted and is boiling. While this is happening, put the lemon juice and egg yolks into a food processor or blender with a good pinch of salt and whizz for 1 minute, to make a pale, thick mixture. With the machine running, pour the melted butter in a steady stream into the food processor or blender through the top of the goblet, and whizz for a further 1 minute.

Let the mixture stand for a minute or two, before serving it with the asparagus.

SERVES 2-4

OPPOSITE: *(left) Asparagus with Hollandaise Sauce and (right) Salad of Bibb Lettuce, Field Lettuce and Herbs*

SALAD OF BIBB LETTUCE, FIELD LETTUCE AND HERBS

Pour 1 tablespoon red wine vinegar, a good pinch of salt, a few grindings of pepper and 3 tablespoons olive oil into a dish and mix together. Then put in 2 tablespoons chopped fresh herbs. Wash 2 heads Bibb lettuce and the field lettuce and pat dry, then tear into pieces and put into the bowl. Just before serving, gently turn the leaves in the dressing, and add 2-4 tablespoons toasted pine nuts.

Field lettuce, or mâche, is available at many fruit and vegetable stores and supermarkets now, and it's also really easy to grow.

SUMMER SPAGHETTI WITH TOMATOES AND BASIL

8 ounces spaghetti or	*sprigs of fresh basil*
whole wheat Chinese	*salt and freshly ground*
noodles	*black pepper*
2 tsp olive oil	*freshly grated*
1 onion, finely chopped	*Parmesan cheese*
4 tomatoes	*(optional)*

Bring a large saucepan two-thirds full of water to a boil. Put in the pasta, easing it down into the water and, when the water comes back to a boil, start timing the pasta: if you're using the whole wheat noodles, cover the pan, take it off the heat, then leave it for 5 minutes.

Meanwhile, heat the oil in a medium saucepan, add the onion, cover and cook for 4 minutes. While the onion is cooking, wash the tomatoes and cut them into eighths, then add them to the onion. Stir-fry them, just to heat them through really.

Drain the pasta into a colander, then put it back into the warm pan and add the tomato mixture, some torn basil leaves and some salt and freshly ground black pepper to taste. Serve at once, with the Parmesan cheese if you're using it.

SERVES 2

FENNEL, TOMATO AND BLACK OLIVE SALAD

I prefer to buy olives loose from a delicatessen or a shop specialising in mediterranean foods.

Put 3 tablespoons olive oil and 1 tablespoon red wine vinegar into a bowl or shallow serving dish, add some salt and pepper and mix together. Wash 2 fennel bulbs and cut off any leafy parts; chop these and add to the oil mixture. If any of the outer layers of the fennel look tough, remove these, then halve the fennel and slice thinly. Wash and slice 4 tomatoes and add the tomato and fennel to the oil mixture, along with 2 tablespoons black olives. Mix gently and leave for at least 30 minutes for the flavors to blend.

RICE SALAD WITH YELLOW AND GREEN ZUCCHINI

The combination of yellow and green zucchini – or baby pattypan squash – makes this a pretty, summery salad. It makes a good light lunch if it's served with a salad, such as Fennel, Tomato and Black Olives, above.

½ cup brown rice	*1 Tbs lemon juice*
2 Tbs wild rice	*grated lemon rind*
8 ounces mixed green	*2 Tbs snipped chives*
and yellow zucchini	*1 Tbs olive oil*
or baby pattypan	*salt and freshly ground*
squash	*black pepper*

Put the brown rice and wild rice into a strainer and wash under cold running water, then put them into a heavy-based saucepan with 1¼ cups water and bring to a boil. Cover the pan and turn the heat down as low as possible; leave the rice to cook, undisturbed, for 40-45 minutes, until all the water has gone and it is tender.

Meanwhile, wash, trim and slice the zucchini or pattypan. Steam them for a few minutes until they are just tender, then remove them from the heat and cover them with cold water to cool them quickly and preserve the color. Drain and pat them dry on paper towels.

When the rice is cooked, stir it gently with a fork, adding the zucchini or pattypan, the lemon juice and a little grated rind to taste, the chives, olive oil and a good seasoning of salt and pepper. Serve as soon as possible, while the salad looks bright and glossy.

SERVES 2 AS A MAIN COURSE, 4 AS A SIDE DISH

TAGLIATELLE OF SUMMER VEGETABLES

A mixture of summer cabbage, zucchini and carrots is good for this; allow about 1½ pounds altogether for four people. Shred the cabbage so that it forms long thin strands, then shave long pieces off the sides of the carrots and zucchini and cut these down to form long, thin strips. Bring half a saucepanful of water to a boil, put in first the carrot, and cook for a minute or two until it begins to get tender, then the cabbage; cook for a further minute, then add the zucchini strands and cook for just 30-60 seconds.

Drain the vegetables, return them to the pan, add a knob of butter, some salt and freshly ground black pepper and perhaps some chopped fresh summer herbs just before serving.

OPPOSITE: *(left) Rice Salad with Yellow and Green Zucchini and (right) Fennel, Tomato and Black Olive Salad*

SUMMER VEGETABLE AND HERB BURGERS

These light, summery burgers are good with a crisp leafy or tomato salad; for a more substantial meal, serve them normal burger-style in a light bun. They need to be eaten as soon as they're cooked as they tend to collapse if kept hot under the broiler or in the oven. You will need a firmish soft white cheese; and ready-grated Parmesan cheese is best for this recipe because of its dryness.

10 green beans	**TO COAT AND FRY**
½ small zucchini	*6 Tbs soft white*
1 cup farmer's cheese	*breadcrumbs*
2 Tbs chopped fresh	*1 Tbs ready-grated*
herbs such as chives,	*Parmesan cheese*
dill, parsley or chervil	*olive oil*
½ cup ready-grated	
Parmesan cheese	
freshly ground black	
pepper	

For a completely food-combining version of the summer vegetable and herb burgers, replace the white breadcrumbs in the coating with very dry ready-grated Parmesan cheese and fry the burgers carefully to maintain their shape.

Wash and trim the green beans then cut them into ½-inch lengths; wash and trim the zucchini and cut into ¼-inch dice. Bring 1 inch of water to a boil in a medium saucepan and put in the green beans; boil for 1 minute, then add the zucchini and boil for 30 seconds. Drain the vegetables into a strainer and refresh them under cold water, then pat dry on paper towels.

Put the farmer's cheese into a bowl and mix in the chopped herbs, then stir in the vegetables, Parmesan cheese and freshly ground black pepper.

To make the coating, mix together the breadcrumbs and the Parmesan cheese on a piece of parchment paper. Divide the farmer's cheese mixture into four and put them on top of the crumb mixture; form into flat round burgers, rolling them in the crumb mixture so that they are well coated. Chill until just before you want to serve them.

To finish the burgers, heat 2 tablespoons of olive oil in a skillet – preferably non-stick – and put in the burgers. Fry them for a minute or two until they are crisp and golden brown on one side, then carefully turn them over and fry them until the other side,

too, is crisp and golden brown, and the inside has heated through. Serve immediately with salad or in buns.
MAKES 4

SPINACH ROULADE WITH MOZZARELLA AND TOMATO FILLING

A spinach roulade is a classic dish which can be varied by using different fillings. I particularly like this version, which is good either hot or cold.

1 pound fresh spinach	**FOR THE FILLING**
or 6 ounces frozen	*10 ounces mozzarella*
1 Tbs butter	*cheese (packed in*
4 eggs, separated	*water)*
salt and freshly ground	*4 medium tomatoes*
black pepper	*3-4 sprigs of fresh*
grated nutmeg	*basil*
4 Tbs ready-grated	
Parmesan cheese	

Set the oven to 400°F. Line a 9 × 13 inch jelly roll pan with parchment paper, to extend a bit up the sides.

If you're using fresh spinach, wash it three times in sinkfuls of cold water, then put it into a large saucepan and cook over a high heat for 7-10 minutes, or until it is very tender. Keep pushing it down into the pan with a slotted spatula as it cooks. Cook frozen spinach in a tiny amount of boiling water, just enough to prevent it from sticking to the pan; it takes about the same length of time. In either case, drain the spinach into a colander and press it very well to extract as much water as possible. Put it into a food processor, along with the butter, egg yolks and a seasoning of salt and freshly ground black pepper and nutmeg, and whizz it all at top speed to make a smooth, creamy-looking purée.

Whisk the egg whites until they stand in stiff peaks, then gently add the spinach mixture and carefully fold it into the egg whites, incorporating it as well as you can without stirring too hard. Tip the mixture into the pan, level the top gently and sprinkle it with 2 tablespoons of the Parmesan. Bake for 10-12 minutes, until the top is springy.

While the roulade is baking, get ready a piece of parchment paper to turn it out on to, by sprinkling it with the rest of the Parmesan. Now prepare the filling: drain the mozzarella and slice thinly; cut the tomatoes into thin rounds and chop the basil.

Take the roulade out of the oven and turn it out on to the parchment paper. Peel the paper off the roulade, cover with a layer of mozzarella slices, then a layer of tomato rounds and finally chopped basil and salt and pepper to taste. Roll up the roulade, starting at one of the long ends. Serve it immediately, or put it on a plate, cover with foil and put it into the oven, turned down to 325°F, for 15 minutes or so.

SERVES 4

TOMATOES STUFFED WITH FLAGEOLETS, WITH RICE

Using canned flageolets makes this a quick and easy dish to make, although you could use dried ones. You would need ½ cup if you were using dried beans; soak them in water for a few hours, then boil them in plenty of water for 45-60 minutes, or until they are tender. If you cook extra for another time, they'll freeze perfectly in a suitable container.

4 large, firm beefsteak tomatoes	1 tsp grated lemon rind
salt and freshly ground black pepper	**FOR THE RICE**
1¾ cups canned flageolets, drained	1 cup brown rice, preferably Basmati
2 Tbs chopped fresh basil	4 Tbs chopped fresh parsley and chives

First, set the oven to 400°F, then put the rice into a medium heavy-based saucepan, add a teaspoonful of salt and 2½ cups of water. Bring to a boil, cover and leave to cook very gently for 30 minutes, or until it's tender and all the water has gone.

Next, prepare the tomatoes. Slice the tops off – the stalks can stay – and scoop out the seeds to make a good cavity for the stuffing. Sprinkle the insides of the tomatoes with salt and pepper. Mix the flageolets with the basil and lemon rind and spoon this mixture into the tomatoes; replace the tops. Put the tomatoes in a shallow casserole and bake them for about 20 minutes, or until they are heated right through but not collapsing.

Finish off the rice by adding the fresh herbs and forking them gently through the rice, fluffing it at the same time. Serve the tomatoes with the rice.

SERVES 4

LETTUCE AND NASTURTIUM BLOSSOM SALAD

This is just a simple salad of lettuce, tossed in a dressing of 1 tablespoon wine vinegar and 3 tablespoons olive oil, plus some salt and pepper, some snipped chives and, added at the last minute just before serving, some bright nasturtium blossoms.

FRUITS, CUPS AND ICES

SUMMER ICE-CREAM CAKE

If you like the idea of this cake but can't face making the ice cream, you can get the same effect by using good-quality bought ice cream, allowing it to soften a bit, then layering it into a pan, freezing and decorating as described in the recipe.

We have a number of summer birthdays in my family and this is a favorite birthday 'cake'.

9 egg yolks
1 cup sugar
3¾ cups heavy cream
4 ounces bittersweet
   chocolate, at least
   50% cocoa solids but
   not a very bitter
   dark one
1 cup strawberries
grated rind of 4 small
   or 2 large oranges

orange food coloring
   (optional)
1 vanilla bean

TO DECORATE
whipped cream
strawberries
chocolate curls
slivers of orange rind
   (optional)

This cake consists of three layers of ice cream: chocolate, orange and strawberry, and real vanilla. Of course you could use different flavorings – puréed raspberries, for a raspberry layer, are good. You make one batch of basic ice cream mixture, then divide it into three portions and add the different flavorings, then set it in layers in a cake pan.

To make the basic ice cream, put the egg yolks into a large bowl or the bowl of an electric beater and whisk until thick and creamy. Put all but 1 tablespoon of the sugar into a small saucepan with 6 tablespoons of water and heat very gently until the sugar has dissolved; turn up the heat and let it bubble for a minute or so until it reaches 225°F on a candy thermometer or a drop of it on the back of the spoon forms a thread when pulled with a teaspoon. (It reaches this stage very quickly.) Immediately remove the pan from the heat and pour the syrup on to the egg yolks while you whisk them. Continue to whisk for 4-5 minutes until the mixture is cool and very thick and creamy. Whip the cream until it holds its shape, then fold it into the egg yolk mixture. Divide the mixture into three roughly equal portions in separate bowls.

For the first layer, break the chocolate into a bowl set over a pan of simmering water and heat gently until it has melted. Stir the melted chocolate into one lot of ice cream. Pour this into the base of an 8-inch deep cake pan and put into the freezer to set, making sure it is standing level.

Hull and dice the strawberries, then put them into a saucepan with the remaining tablespoonful of sugar. Heat gently until the sugar has dissolved and the strawberries are tender: 5-10 minutes. Cool. Add the grated orange rind to the second bowl of ice cream, and intensify the coloring a bit if you like with orange food coloring. Gently fold in the strawberries. If you have room in your freezer, this can go into the freezer for the moment. For the final ice cream, split the vanilla bean and scrape the gooey black seeds out of the skin, using half or all of the bean to taste. Add this vanilla to the final bowl of ice cream and put that, too, into the freezer.

After about 30 minutes, or when the chocolate layer of ice cream has begun to set, gently spoon the orange and strawberry ice cream on top, in an even layer, and put the pan back into the freezer for another 15-30 minutes, or until the orange layer is beginning to get firm. Then scoop the final layer on top, beating it a bit if it has set round the edges. Smooth the top and leave to set completely.

To finish the cake, have ready some whipped cream in a pastry bag fitted with a medium shell tube. Take the ice-cream cake out of the freezer and run the blade of a knife around the edges, invert the cake on to a suitable plate – give it a shake and the cake should come out. Pipe a little cream around the edges and in the center, then put the cake back in the freezer and open-freeze it until required. Or decorate it straight away, with strawberries with their stems still attached, chocolate curls and slivers of orange rind, if using. Serve immediately.
SERVES 12

OPPOSITE: *Summer Ice-Cream Cake*

STRAWBERRIES IN CHOCOLATE CASES

You need a good quality chocolate for the cases, but not a very bitter dark one. The cases need to be made a few hours in advance, to give them time to set, but not overnight as they gradually become dull.

FOR THE CASES

7 ounces bittersweet chocolate, at least 50% cocoa solids

FOR THE FILLING

1½ cups strawberries
about 3 Tbs cherry and red currant sugar-free preserves or red currant jelly

TO SERVE (OPTIONAL)

raspberry coulis, see right
a few strawberry leaves to decorate

First make the chocolate cases which need to be done a few hours in advance. Break the chocolate into a bowl set over a pan of simmering water and heat gently to melt. Have ready some fluted paper cups. Using two cups together for firmness, coat the inside quite thickly with melted chocolate. Repeat with all the cups then leave them for 30-60 minutes to set. Give them all another coat of chocolate, making sure it's quite thick around the rim, as this is where it tends to break. Leave them for several hours to firm up, then peel off the paper cups and put the chocolate cases on individual plates.

Hull, wash and slice the strawberries, then put a few in each chocolate case, piling them up attractively. Gently melt the sugar-free preserves or red currant jelly and spoon a little on top of the strawberries, being careful not to get the hot jelly on the chocolate. Serve with the raspberry coulis if you are using this, and decorate with the strawberry leaves.
SERVES 6

OPPOSITE: *(left) Rose Petal Creams and (right) Strawberries in Chocolate Cases*

ROSE PETAL CREAMS

Rosewater is available from gourmet markets and middle eastern food stores.

1¼ cups plain low-fat yogurt
1¼ cups heavy cream
2-3 tsp rosewater

superfine sugar or clear honey
1½ cups raspberries
rose petals to decorate

Put the yogurt and cream into a bowl and whisk together until the mixture is thick. Add the rosewater and a little sugar or clear honey to taste. Wash the raspberries and pat them dry very gently with paper towels, then sprinkle them with a little superfine sugar to sweeten them as necessary.

Spoon layers of raspberries and the rose cream into six deep glasses, starting with raspberries, then cream, followed by more raspberries, and a final layer of cream. Cover and chill until needed. Scatter some pink rose petals on top before serving.

The petals can be crystallized first by coating them with lightly beaten egg white, then sprinkling all over with superfine sugar and leaving to dry on a rack covered with parchment paper.
SERVES 4

To make raspberry coulis, purée 2 cups fresh or frozen raspberries in a blender with 2 tbs water, then pass through a strainer. Add sugar as necessary to taste.

THE ULTIMATE PEACH MELBA

*raspberry coulis (see
   page 63)*
6 large, perfect peaches
*¼-½ cup slivered
   almonds*

1 vanilla bean
1 egg yolk
*½ cup superfine
   sugar*
1¼ cups heavy cream

**FOR THE VANILLA ICE
CREAM**

1¼ cups milk

First make the ice cream. Put the milk into a saucepan with the vanilla bean and bring to a boil. Meanwhile, mix the egg yolk with the sugar. Pour the boiling milk over the egg yolk mixture, stir, then return the whole lot to the saucepan. Stir over a gentle heat for a minute or two until the mixture thickens slightly and will coat the back of the spoon thinly – don't let it boil. Remove from the heat immediately and cool. (You can hasten this process by transferring the mixture to a bowl and standing it in another bowl of cold water.)

Put the cream into a large bowl and whisk until it forms soft peaks, then gradually whisk in the cooled egg yolk mixture. If you have an ice-cream maker, pour the mixture into that and freeze it according to the instructions. If not, pour it into a suitable container to freeze – or freeze it in the bowl, if your freezer is big enough. As it freezes, beat the mixture every half hour or so if you can, to break up the ice crystals and make a very smooth ice cream. (It's helpful if you freeze the ice cream in the bowl, or in a container which you can beat it in, to avoid having to keep transferring it from container to bowl.) Once it's frozen, keep it in a covered container in the freezer. Remove it from the freezer 45 minutes before you want to serve it, to allow it to soften up.

Next, make the raspberry coulis according to recipe instructions and set aside until you need it.

Just before you want to serve the dessert, prepare the peaches by putting them into a bowl, pouring boiling water over them and leaving them for 30-60 seconds, or until the skins will slip off.

Remove all the skins, halve the peaches and remove the pits. Put two peach halves on each plate, top with a scoop of ice cream, spoon some raspberry coulis over the top and sprinkle with some slivered almonds. Serve at once.
SERVES 6

SOFT CHEESE SUMMER MOLD

I wanted to see if I could make this summer mold with a difference. I had decided to make an outside shell of soft cheese, with a luscious filling of red summer fruits, but for a long time I couldn't think how to make it so that the cheese could drain. Then I hit on the idea of using a round strainer lined with cheesecloth. It worked perfectly, resulting in this delicious summer mold which we found delectable. It's best to start the preparation the day before, or a few hours before the mold is needed.

*1½ cups farmer's cheese
   or other soft white
   skim milk cheese*
⅞ cup heavy cream
3 Tbs sugar
*1 pint mixed red
   summer fruit*

*4 Tbs cherry and red
   currant sugar-free
   preserves*
*a few strawberries to
   decorate*

First, line a 6½-inch-diameter round strainer with a piece of cheesecloth and set it over a bowl so that it isn't touching the base. Next, put the soft white cheese and the heavy cream into a bowl with the sugar and whisk until the mixture is stiff but not breaking up. Spoon a good two-thirds of it into the cheesecloth-lined strainer and press it down, so that it forms an even layer.

Wash, hull and slice the fruit as necessary, then mix it with the sugar-free preserves to sweeten it. Spoon the mixture into the strainer on top of the soft cheese, then spread the rest of the cheese mixture evenly over the top. Cover with several layers of paper towels, then a plate and a weight, and leave for several hours or overnight. The soft cheese will drip into the bowl and firm up.

To serve the mold, remove the paper towels and invert the strainer over a serving plate. Turn out the mold, then gently remove the cheesecloth. Decorate with some strawberries with their stalks still attached.

SERVES 6

CHOCOLATE TRUFFLE CAKE WITH CHERRIES IN KIRSCH

This is a very indulgent but wonderful dessert.

8 ounces bittersweet chocolate, at least 50% cocoa solids
2 Tbs butter
1¼ cups heavy cream
2 pounds ripe sweet red cherries

4 Tbs kirsch
sugar to taste
2 ounces bittersweet chocolate, grated whipping cream to serve

First of all, line an 8-inch shallow cake pan with a circle of parchment paper. Break the chocolate into a bowl and add the butter; set the bowl over a pan of simmering water and heat gently for a few minutes until the chocolate and butter have melted. Remove from the heat and leave to cool slightly.

Meanwhile, whisk the cream until it will hold a shape but is not too stiff, then gently fold it into the chocolate. Pour this mixture into the pan and smooth the top. Cover and leave to chill and set for several hours. While the cream is chilling, wash and pit the cherries and put them into a bowl with the kirsch and just a little sugar to taste if necessary. Cover and leave until required.

Just before you want to serve the truffle cake, turn it out on to a plate – if you first loosen the edges, then put a plate over it and give it a good

shake, it should come out all right. Cover the top with a thick layer of grated chocolate. Serve with the cherries, and some extra softly whipped cream.

SERVES 6

SUMMER BERRIES WITH SABAYON SAUCE

4 egg yolks
¼ cup sugar
2 Tbs Cointreau or other orange liqueur

⅔ cup heavy cream, whipped
1½ cups raspberries, strawberries and a little extra sugar

Put the egg yolks into a bowl set over a pan of simmering water, making sure that the base of the bowl doesn't touch the water. Add the sugar to the yolks and whisk until the mixture is very thick and creamy: this will take at least 10 minutes so it helps if you have an electric hand beater. Remove the bowl from the heat and leave it to cool, whisking it often. Stir in the Cointreau and gently fold in the cream. Chill until required.

To finish the dessert, wash, hull and slice the fruit as necessary; spoon a pool of the sauce on to four plates, then put the red fruits in the center and sprinkle with a little sugar.

SERVES 4

A classic sabayon sauce makes a delectable accompaniment for summer berries.

SUMMER MENUS

MENU

A PERFECT SUMMER LUNCH IN THE GARDEN FOR FOUR

Little Pea and Mint Custards

Summer Salad Roulade with Fresh Herb Sauce
Little New Potatoes Baked in a Parcel
Green Bean Vinaigrette

Jellied Terrine of Red Summer Fruits
Orange Ice Cream with Pistachio Nuts

COUNTDOWN

Up to 1 week in advance:
Make the Orange and Pistachio Ice Cream.

Up to one day before:
Make the Little Pea and Mint Custards, the Jellied
Red Fruit Terrine, the Fresh Herb Sauce and the
Green Bean Vinaigrette, cover and keep in the fridge.

1-2 hours before:
Make and fill the Roulade if you are going to serve
this warm; it can be done 3-4 hours in advance if you
are planning to serve it cold. Heat the oven so that it is
ready 35 minutes before you want to eat the meal,
then prepare and bake the potatoes in their parcel.

LITTLE PEA AND MINT CUSTARDS

Delicate in texture, flavor and appearance, these little savory custards are a real lunchtime treat. I usually make them in dariole molds of ⅔-cup capacity, but little ramekins or custard cups would be good alternatives.

1½ cups shelled fresh peas	*2 eggs*
butter and ready-grated Parmesan cheese for preparing the molds	*2 egg yolks*
	⅔ cup light cream
	4 Tbs heavy cream
	salt and freshly ground black pepper
sprigs of fresh mint	

Set the oven to 325°F.

Cook the peas in boiling water for a few minutes until they are tender, then drain. While the peas are cooking, grease four molds well with butter and sprinkle with the Parmesan cheese.

Put the drained peas into a food processor with 3 good sprigs of mint and whizz to a purée then push the mixture through a strainer into a bowl. Add the eggs, yolks and creams and whisk well. Season with salt and freshly ground black pepper. Pour into the molds, put them into a small roasting pan and pour boiling water around them to come at least halfway up their sides. Bake for about 35 minutes, or until they feel set, and a wooden toothpick inserted into the center of one comes out clean.

Turn them out on to warmed plates, if you want to serve them hot; otherwise let them cool in their molds. I think they're best just warm. They should come out of the molds all right if you loosen the edges with a knife then, holding them over a plate, give them a shake. Garnish with mint.

OPPOSITE: *Dishes from a Perfect Summer Lunch in the Garden for Four*

SUMMER SALAD ROULADE WITH FRESH HERB SAUCE

This light roulade can be served warm or cold; it's good either way.

butter for greasing and
ready-grated
Parmesan cheese for
coating
¼ cup farmer's cheese
4 eggs, separated
⅔ cup light cream
2 cups grated Gruyère
cheese

salt and freshly ground
black pepper

FOR THE FILLING
2 heaping Tbs
mayonnaise
3 floppy lettuce leaves
2 tomatoes, skinned
2 scallions, finely
chopped

Accompany this lunch with an aromatic or medium-bodied dry white wine such as a Sancerre or Frascati; or try a dry rosé.

Set the oven to 400°F. Line a 13 × 9 inch jelly roll pan with a piece of parchment paper – it needn't be too tidy. Grease the paper and sprinkle with the grated Parmesan cheese.

Put the farmer's cheese and egg yolks into a large bowl and mix together until smooth, then gradually mix in the cream; finally, stir in the grated Gruyère cheese. In another bowl, whisk the egg whites until they're stiff, then fold these into the Gruyère mixture. Season as necessary with salt and pepper.

Pour the mixture into the lined pan, smoothing it gently to the edges and making sure it's even. Bake for 12-15 minutes, until risen and just firm in the center. Remove from the oven. Have ready a piece of parchment paper spread out on the work surface and sprinkled with ready-grated Parmesan cheese. Turn the roulade straight out, face-down, on to the parchment paper. Cover with a clean, slightly damp dish towel and leave to cool. (It needs to be cool enough not to wilt the salad filling.)

Spread the cooled roulade with the mayonnaise, then put the lettuce leaves on top. Slice the tomatoes very thinly and put these on top of the lettuce, and finally the scallions and some salt and pepper. Roll up the roulade, starting from one of the long edges – it's easiest to do this if you first make an incision about ½ inch from the edge (but don't cut

right through) then bend this down to start the rolling process. Use the paper to help you to roll it firmly. Transfer the roulade to a long serving dish and serve with the herb sauce, potatoes and green beans suggested below.

FRESH HERB SAUCE

For the herb sauce, stir 1¼ cups plain low-fat yogurt until it's smooth, then mix in 2 tablespoons each of snipped chives and parsley; add salt and freshly ground black pepper to taste.

LITTLE NEW POTATOES BAKED IN A PARCEL

Based on Elizabeth David's recipe in *French Country Cooking*, this is one of the easiest and most delicious ways of preparing new potatoes. Scrub or scrape 24 very small new potatoes, then put them on to a piece of parchment paper with 2 mint leaves, 4 Tbs butter and 2 pinches of salt. Fold the paper over, then fold down the edges so that the potatoes are securely sealed. Bake in the oven at 375°F for 35 minutes.

GREEN BEAN VINAIGRETTE

Top and tail 1-1½ pounds green beans, the thinner the better. Boil them in 1 inch of water for 3-4 minutes, or steam them for perhaps a minute or two longer, until they have cooked a little but are still quite crisp. Drain them immediately and put them into a bowl with 1 tablespoon wine vinegar, 2 tablespoons olive oil and some salt and pepper. Leave to cool, stirring them from time to time. Serve warm or cold.

JELLIED TERRINE OF RED SUMMER FRUITS

In this glistening red terrine, strawberries are layered with a fruit spread which holds them together and sets them without gelatin. It can be made a few hours in advance and kept very cold until needed, but only turn it out a moment or two before serving. After the first slice has been cut it will collapse, although it will still taste wonderful. I think something sharp goes well with it – crème fraîche or thick yogurt.

1½ pints ripe but firm strawberries
about 1½ cups cherry and red currant sugar-free preserves

fresh mint leaves and summer fruits to decorate (optional)

Hull, wash and dry the strawberries, then cut them into thin slices. Melt the cherry and red currant sugar-free preserves in a saucepan and pour a little into the base of a small loaf pan, just enough to coat the base by about ⅛ inch. Leave it for a minute or two to begin to set, then put a layer of strawberry slices in on top. Pour in a little more of the melted preserves, top with more strawberries, and continue in this way until all the strawberries and preserves are used up and the pan is full. Leave to cool, then chill thoroughly.

A minute or two before you want to serve the terrine, slip the blade of a knife around the edges and invert the pan on to a serving plate, giving it a shake. Decorate with a few mint leaves and summer fruits, if using. Serve immediately.

ORANGE ICE CREAM WITH PISTACHIO NUTS

The flavor of orange goes well with red summer fruits, and this ice cream makes a good accompaniment for the Jellied Terrine of Red Summer Fruits. Pistachio nuts add a pleasant touch of color and texture to the ice cream, although you could leave them out if you prefer.

You can get shelled Pistachio nuts at some supermarkets and these are fine for this recipe.

2 medium oranges
½ cup sugar
4 egg yolks
1¼ cups heavy cream

½ cup shelled pistachio nuts, quite coarsely chopped

Scrub one of the oranges in hot water, then dry it and grate off the rind finely. Squeeze the juice from both the oranges: you should have about ⅔ cup. Put the orange juice into a small saucepan with the sugar and heat gently until the sugar has dissolved; then let it boil for about 4 minutes, until the mixture reaches 225°F on a candy thermometer or a little of the syrup forms a thread when pulled between your finger and thumb.

Meanwhile, whisk the egg yolks until they are beginning to thicken: it's easiest to do this with an electric mixer if you have one. Pour the orange syrup on top of the egg yolks, whisking at the same time, and continue to whisk for about 5 minutes, until the mixture is thick and pale. Whip the cream until it holds its shape then fold this into the orange mixture, along with the pistachio nuts.

Transfer the mixture to a suitable container and freeze until firm. This ice cream doesn't need stirring as it freezes, but let it stand at room temperature for 30 minutes before you want to eat it to give it a chance to soften up, and give it a stir before serving. Alternatively, do this beforehand and put scoops of ice cream on to a plate, then refreeze so that you can serve it quickly and easily later.

——— COUNTDOWN ———

Up to several hours in advance:
Prepare the Polenta ready for grilling (this can
be done a day ahead if convenient). Make the Tomato
Sauce, Garlic Cream, Onion Salsa and Fruit
and Flower Compôte. Cover them all tightly and
keep in the fridge. Wash the salad and
put that in a plastic bag in the fridge, too.

1 hour ahead:
Prepare the radicchio, eggplant and Haloumi cheese
ready for grilling. Light the barbecue about 40
minutes before you want to start cooking. Dress and
toss the salad at the last minute; reheat the
Tomato Sauce. Grill the eggplant, Haloumi
cheese, polenta, fennel and radicchio on the barbecue.

GRILLED EGGPLANT WITH HALOUMI CHEESE, AND TOMATO SAUCE

*You can get Haloumi cheese at large supermarkets.
You need to read the packets, because some batches
are made with animal rennet and some are not.
Haloumi cheese keeps for months in the fridge and it
also freezes. Its unusual, firm texture makes it excellent for frying, broiling and barbecuing.*

2 large eggplants
1 pound Haloumi
  cheese
olive oil
cherry tomatoes to
  garnish

FOR THE SAUCE
2 Tbs olive oil

2 onions, peeled and
  sliced
2-4 garlic cloves,
  crushed
4 thin slices of lemon
3½ cups canned
  tomatoes
chili powder
salt and freshly ground
  black pepper

First make the sauce, which can be done well in
advance. Heat the oil in a large saucepan and put in
the onions; cover and cook gently for 5 minutes,
add the garlic and lemon slices, cover and cook for
a further 5 minutes. Put in the tomatoes, with their
liquid, and a good pinch of chili powder, and cook
uncovered for about 10 minutes, until much of the
liquid has disappeared. Purée the mixture, including the lemon, in a blender. Taste and add salt and
pepper, and more chili powder, as necessary.

Cut the eggplants into slices just less than ½ inch
thick, aiming for 16 good slices. If you like,
sprinkle them with salt in a colander and leave for
30 minutes, then rinse under cold running water to
remove any bitterness, though I have never come
across a bitter eggplant. Cut the Haloumi cheese
into similar slices.

Oil a cookie sheet and heat under a broiler, then
put slices of eggplant on to this or straight on to a
hot oiled barbecue grid and turn them over, so that
both surfaces get oiled. Then grill, first on one side

OPPOSITE: *A Family Barbecue for Eight to Ten*

and then on the other, until the eggplant is lightly browned. Put the slices on to a warm plate and quickly grill the cheese in the same way (or do the eggplant slices and the cheese slices at the same time if your cookie sheet or grid is large). When both sides of the cheese are flecked with brown and the cheese is crisping at the edges, lift the slices off the cookie sheet or barbecue grid with a metal spatula and put one on each slice of eggplant. Garnish with the cherry tomatoes and serve with the sauce.

CHICK-PEA POLENTA WITH TOMATO AND ONION SALSA

Beer and wine both go well with this menu. My personal choice would be a chilled light fruity wine such as a Beaujolais.

Chick-pea flour can be cooked and made into slices in exactly the same way as polenta flour, but I prefer the chick-pea version. These slices can be fried, deep-fried or broiled, and (possibly without the cumin seeds) are enormously popular with kids and teenagers. They make ideal vegetarian barbecue food and I think they're enhanced by a bit of charring and wood-smoke flavors. The kids tend to smother them with ketchup, but I think a simple salsa, made from tomatoes and fresh cilantro, goes best with them. You can get chick-pea flour at health stores or Middle Eastern and Indian stores. It may be called Besan or Gram flour.

1½ cups chick-pea flour	olive oil
2 tsp salt	1 Tbs cumin seeds
	slices of lemon

Sift the chick-pea flour and salt into a medium saucepan and mix to a smooth paste with 2½ cups of cold water. Put the pan on the heat and stir gently until the mixture comes to a boil and is thick and smooth. Let it cook gently, heaving and bubbling a bit, for about 10 minutes, until it's very thick, and any raw flavor has gone. Turn the mixture out on to a piece of parchment paper, spread-

ing it to a depth of about ⅓ inch or a bit less. Leave it to get cold – or for several hours if you wish – then cut it into rectangles or other shapes. (The shapes can be open-frozen at this point and can later be cooked from frozen.)

Put the shapes on a broiler pan or on a barbecue grid that has been greased with olive oil, then turn them, so that they are oiled all over. Sprinkle the cumin seeds on top, then grill the polenta for a few minutes on each side, until they are bubbling, flecked with brown and crisp at the edges. They may seem a bit soft when you turn them, but they'll crisp up as the second side cooks and should prove quite manageable as long as you have a good slotted spatula to turn them with. Serve with slices of lemon and tomato and onion salsa.

TOMATO AND ONION SALSA

Fry 1 mild onion, peeled and sliced, gently in a little oil for 7 minutes, until almost tender. Halve, seed and finely chop a green chili, being careful not to get the juice anywhere near your eyes and to wash your hands afterwards. Add the chili to the onion and fry for a further 2-3 minutes, then remove from the heat and put the mixture into a bowl.

Peel 2 pounds tomatoes by covering them with boiling water, leaving for 60 seconds, then draining and slipping off the skins with a sharp knife. Chop the tomatoes coarsely, discarding any tough bits of stem, and add the tomatoes to the bowl. Pare off one or two strips of rind from a lime and snip them into shreds; squeeze the juice from the lime. Add to the tomatoes, with about 4-6 tablespoons chopped cilantro leaves and some salt and pepper.

GRILLED FENNEL AND RADICCHIO WITH GARLIC CREAM

4 fennel bulbs
2 radicchio
olive oil
salt and freshly ground
  black pepper
lemon slices or fresh
  herb sprigs to garnish

FOR THE GARLIC CREAM
1¼ cups garlic-and-
  herb-flavored Boursin
  cheese

The garlic cream can be made in advance and kept in a covered dish in the fridge. To make it, simply mash the garlic-and-herb-flavored cream cheese to break it up and beat in ½ cup hot water to make a smooth, creamy mixture.

To prepare the vegetables, trim the fennel and radicchio, removing any tough leaves and pieces of stem but leaving enough of the stem to hold the leaves together at the base. Cut each down first into halves, then into quarters and eighths, so that they are still joined together at the base if possible. Steam or parboil the fennel for about 8 minutes, or until it is just tender without being at all soggy. Drain well and dry with paper towels.

Brush both the fennel and the radicchio with oil and sprinkle with some salt and pepper, then cook them over hot coals until they are lightly charred on both sides: this will take about 5-8 minutes on a barbecue and slightly longer, about 15 minutes, under a broiler. They can be served warm, like a salad, so can be done ahead of the other barbecue items if more convenient. Garnish them with lemon slices and serve them with the garlic cream sauce.

SUMMER LEAF SALAD

This salad is never the same twice, because you can put in whatever leaves and herbs happen to be available. Sometimes I've made it with just garden lettuce and as many different herbs as I could add, but it's more interesting when you can use a good variety of greens. When they're available, I like to put in tender dandelion and nasturtium greens, baby spinach leaves, arugula, field lettuce and any red, curly or fancy-leaf lettuce, as well as the basic type.

1 head Boston or Bibb
  lettuce
1 head curly endive or
  oak-leaf lettuce
arugula, nasturtium,
  dandelion, spinach
  and field lettuce, as
  available

FOR THE DRESSING
2 Tbs red wine vinegar
6 Tbs olive oil
salt and freshly ground
  black pepper
4 Tbs chopped fresh
  herbs such as chives,
  mint, parsley, basil,
  dill, as available

Wash the lettuces and other greens and shake or spin them dry. Make the dressing straight into the bowl from which you want to serve the salad. Put the vinegar and oil into the bowl with a good seasoning of salt and freshly ground black pepper and mix them until they emulsify; then stir in the chopped herbs.

Put the salad greens in on top of the dressing, tearing them into manageable sizes as you do so. Toss the salad at the last minute, just before you want to serve it, so that the leaves are all crisp and lightly coated with the herb vinaigrette.

FRUIT AND FLOWER COMPOTE IN ROSEHIP TEA

The tea gives this compôte an intriguing flavor. Look for tea bags which contain both rosehip and hibiscus; the ones I particularly like are flavored with raspberry, too.

2¼ cups cherry and red currant sugar-free preserves

6 rosehip, hibiscus and raspberry tea bags

8 ripe nectarines

rose petals and a few small summer flowers such as borage, lavender, pinks

Put the sugar-free preserves into a saucepan with 1 cup water and the tea bags, and heat gently until the spread has melted. Remove from the heat and tip the mixture into a large bowl.

Wash the nectarines, then cut them into thin slices, discarding the pits. Add the slices to the bowl and mix well. Cover and leave for at least an hour for all the flavors to develop.

Just before serving the fruit salad, remove the tea bags, squeezing all the liquid out of them and adding this to the fruit salad. Serve the compôte in a shallow glass bowl with the petals and flowers scattered on top.

BLACKBERRY FOOL

The sweeter the blackberries are the better, because you'll need to add less sugar.

1 pound blackberries

1-2 Tbs cherry and red currant sugar-free preserves

⅔ cup low-fat plain yogurt

⅔ cup heavy cream

sugar to taste

Wash the blackberries, then put them into a saucepan with the fruit spread and cook over a gentle heat for a few minutes until the juices run and the blackberries are very tender. Pureé the blackberries in a food processor, then push this pureé through a nylon strainer to remove the seeds.

When the mixture is cool, reserve about two tablespoons of the blackberry mixture and stir the yogurt into the rest, then whisk the cream and fold that into the mixture. Taste and add a little sugar if necessary. Divide the fool between four bowls and spoon the reserved blackberry mixture on top.
SERVES 4

OPPOSITE: *Fruit and Flower Compôte in Rosehip Tea*

FALL

FALL

The heat of summer gives way to the mellowness of fall. The days become shorter and the path of the sun gets lower in the sky, crossing the equator at the time of the fall equinox. The harvest, the precious fruits and vegetables, grains and seeds which will sustain us throughout the darkest months of the year, is gathered in. The life-processes begin to wane, the sap flows less strongly, the leaves become vibrant shades of yellow, gold and red, then drop to the ground as the earth moves to a state of peace and rest. In the country there's the smell of wood smoke in the air, the mornings are misty and cobwebs sparkle in the dew.

During the fall, certain festivals stand out. The gathering in of the harvest, Thanksgiving, and Halloween are all linked in that they remind us that there are other dimensions to life apart from the physical. This is a time of the year I particularly like, because the world of spirit seems much closer than usual. There is a good astrological reason for this since they all happen during the time when the sun is in Scorpio, the sign which is associated with death, the after-life and the world of spirit. Scorpio is the opposite sign to Taurus, and both signs belong to the fixed element, which accounts for the feeling of underlying peace and stability during this season when in one instance there is the resurgence of life and on the other, the waning: opposite sides of the perpetual cycle of life.

Fall, like spring, is a time of change, a transition from the heat and sunshine of summer to the cold of winter. Some fall days can be surprisingly hot, and an Indian summer has its special joy and poignancy; but the breeze has an increasingly cool edge to it. Late

summer/early fall vegetables such as bell peppers, eggplants, artichokes and fennel bridge the gap between summer and winter admirably, being substantial yet not stodgy; pumpkin, leeks, mushrooms and celery root also have this quality. All these vegetables are welcome as far as I am concerned, although I have a special affection for pumpkin, with its glorious color, light texture, delicate flavor and its association with Halloween. As the season advances and we experience the first frosts, heavier, more sustaining foods become available: the first of the fall root vegetables, the new-season pulses; nuts, with their concentrated nutrients, their warming and protective oils.

As the nights draw in, it seems a natural time to have informal get-togethers, parties and harvest suppers, and welcoming bakes and gratins made from fall vegetables are an easy and popular way to cater for them; dishes like Eggplant, Tomato and Mozzarella Bake (page 102), Pumpkin and Goat Cheese Gratin (page 84) and Spaghetti Squash with Gorgonzola, Cream and Walnuts (page 89). And fall fruits, especially apples, pears, plums and damsons, with their earthy fragrances and flavors, make wonderful seasonal desserts.

Fall is also the time to hunt for edible treasures in the fields and woods: blackberries, chestnuts, hazel or cob nuts and walnuts on the trees, and funghi on the ground. Going on a mushroom hunt armed with a couple of reliable guidebooks can be well rewarded, although you need a certain amount of courage to try the results unless you have an expert with you, or can have them expertly identified. Anyway, whether you manage to find any wild mushrooms or just buy them from a shop, having a feast of funghi is one of the delights of the season.

SEASONAL APPETIZERS

PEARS IN TARRAGON VINAIGRETTE

The success of this simple, refreshing appetizer depends on using perfect pears, ripe enough to slice with a spoon. I find it best to buy them several days before I need them and let them ripen to the right point. Comice pears give the best result.

3 ripe comice pears	*several sprigs of fresh*
2 Tbs tarragon vinegar	*tarragon*
2 Tbs light olive oil	*oak leaf or red curly*
salt and freshly ground	*leaf lettuce*
black pepper	

Quarter and peel the pears, removing the core, cut them into pieces and put them into a shallow dish.

Put the vinegar, oil and some salt into a jar and shake together until blended, then pour over the pears. Chop the tarragon – there should be 2-3 tablespoonfuls – and add to the pears. Coarsely grind plenty of pepper on top, and stir the mixture gently; if possible leave it for at least 30 minutes for the flavors to develop and blend.

To serve, arrange a few torn leaves of oak leaf or red curly leaf lettuce on four plates and spoon the pieces of pear and their juice on top.
SERVES 4

Buy walnuts from a shop which has a quick turnover so that they will be really fresh with no hint of bitterness.

HOT CELERY ROOT PUREE ON A BED OF WATERCRESS

This was one of those mixtures which happened almost by accident, because of the ingredients I happened to have in, and which turned out to be really good. The combination of hot creamy celery root purée, cool, crisp, peppery watercress and walnuts is extremely good.

1½ pounds celery root	*½ cup fresh shelled*
1 Tbs butter	*walnuts*
2-3 Tbs cream	*bunch of watercress*
salt and freshly ground	*(about 3 cups)*
black pepper	*3 Tbs walnut oil*
	1 Tbs red wine vinegar

Peel the celery root, then cut it into even-sized chunks. Put them into a saucepan, cover with water, and boil for about 15 minutes, or until the chunks are tender when pierced with a knife. Drain – the water makes a superb stock, I always save it – then mash the celery root with the butter, cream and salt and pepper to taste.

While the celery root is cooking, chop the walnuts roughly, then wash the watercress and remove any tough stems. Mix the oil, vinegar and some salt and pepper in a bowl, add the watercress and mix.

To serve, divide the watercress between four plates, put a mound of the celery root on top and sprinkle with the walnuts.
SERVES 4

OPPOSITE: *(left) Pears in Tarragon Vinaigrette and (right) Hot Celery Root Purée*

FRIED PUMPKIN SLICES WITH DEEP-FRIED SAGE

Thinly sliced pumpkin, fried in olive oil until it is crisp on the outside, tender within, makes a quick, good appetizer. The crisp, deep-fried sage makes an attractive garnish, and is quick to do.

a little oil for deep-frying	**4 garlic cloves, peeled**
12 sprigs of fresh sage	**olive oil**
1¼ pounds pumpkin, weighed with skin and seeds	**coarse salt**
	freshly grated Parmesan cheese (optional)

Coarse sea salt is my favorite with its crunchy flakes that you don't need to grind. It can be bought from health stores and large supermarkets.

First prepare the deep-fried sage for the garnish. Heat 1 inch of oil in a small saucepan. When it is sizzling hot, put in some of the sage sprigs and deep-fry for a minute or two until they are crunchy, then drain them on paper towels and repeat the process with the rest. Keep on one side until required.

Peel the skin from the piece of pumpkin and remove all the seeds and threads. Cut the pumpkin flesh into long slim pieces something like 4 inches by 1-1½ inches, and not more than ¼ inch thick. Crush the garlic cloves to a paste in some coarse salt. With a knife, smear this garlic paste very thinly on each side of the pumpkin slices to flavor them lightly.

Heat a little olive oil in a skillet, and fry the pumpkin slices for about 3 minutes on each side, or until they are lightly browned and crisp and feel tender when pierced with the point of a knife. Take them out and drain them on paper towels. Serve them as soon as possible on warmed plates, sprinkled with a little crunchy coarse salt and garnished with the deep-fried sage. Hand round the Parmesan cheese separately if you're serving this.
SERVES 4

FENNEL A LA GRECQUE

Pleasant either warm or chilled, this is good served with some bread to mop up the juices.

4 fennel bulbs	**1¾ cups canned**
2 tbs olive oil	**tomatoes**
1 tbs coriander seeds	**salt and freshly ground**
4 strips of lemon peel	**black pepper**
juice of 1 lemon	

Trim the fennel, saving any leafy bits. Pare off any chunky root part, and if the outer leaves look tough, either remove them or pare them a bit with a sharp knife, depending on how edible they look. Then cut the fennel down into eighths.

Heat the oil in a heavy-based saucepan and put in the fennel; turn it so that it all gets coated with the oil, then cover the pan and leave it to cook gently while you crush the coriander seeds roughly. A pestle and mortar is best for doing this; otherwise improvise by putting them into a small bowl and crushing them with the end of something like a rolling pin. Add the seeds to the fennel, along with the lemon peel and juice, and stir again.

Chop the tomatoes roughly then add them, and their juice, to the pan. Mix gently, cover and leave to cook gently for 15-20 minutes, or until the fennel is very tender and the tomato is reduced to a glistening crimson sauce. Remove from the heat, season with salt and pepper and leave to cool.

Add the reserved fennel leaves, chopped, just before serving.
SERVES 4

GOLDEN BELL PEPPERS STUFFED WITH CHERRY TOMATOES

This is a pretty appetizer – red cherry tomatoes and green basil in golden bell pepper halves – and it's also easy to do. If you can't get cherry tomatoes, it can also be made successfully with ordinary tomatoes, chopped. It is equally good served as it is, or it can be lightly cooked.

2 golden bell peppers
8 ounces cherry
  tomatoes
1-2 tbs chopped fresh
  basil

salt and freshly ground
  black pepper
olive oil (optional)

If you're planning to cook this appetizer, set the oven to 400°F.

Halve the bell peppers, cutting through the stems and leaving these attached, then put the peppers shiny-side up on a broiler pan and broil at full heat until the skin has blistered and begun to char. Move them halfway through the broiling so that all the skin gets done. Cover them with a plate to keep in the steam, and leave until they're cool enough to handle. Slip off the skins with a sharp knife – they'll come off easily – and rinse the bell peppers under cold water to remove the seeds. Finally, put them, the other way up this time, in a shallow casserole.

Peel the tomatoes by covering them with boiling water, leaving them for a few seconds until their skins loosen, then draining them and slipping off the skins. Halve or quarter the tomatoes, depending on their size, and mix them with the basil and some salt and pepper. Spoon this mixture into the bell pepper halves, dividing it between them. Trickle a little olive oil over each if you wish.

Serve the bell peppers as they are, or put them into the oven and bake them for 15-20 minutes.
SERVES 4

SWEET POTATOES WITH HERB STUFFING

3 medium sweet
  potatoes, about
  10 ounces each
2 tbs butter
2 tbs snipped chives

1½ tsp chopped fresh
  thyme
salt and freshly ground
  black pepper

Set the oven to 400°F. Wash and prick the sweet potatoes. Place them on a cookie sheet and bake for about 1 hour, or until they feel soft when squeezed. Holding them in a cloth, cut them in half horizontally, then scoop out the flesh into a basin with a teaspoon, being careful not to break the skins. Choose four of the best skins and place them in a baking dish, discarding the rest.

Add the butter to the scooped-out sweet potato flesh and mash well, then add the chives, thyme and salt and pepper. Spoon the mixture into the skins, piling them up well, then put them back into the oven for about 15 minutes to heat through.

They can be prepared in advance and heated through just before serving; if heating them through from cold, allow a bit longer: 20-25 minutes.
SERVES 4

WARMING MEALS

PUMPKIN AND GOAT CHEESE GRATIN

I love the contrast of the sharp flavor of the goat cheese and the sweet creaminess of the pumpkin in this easy gratin. I like to serve it with the Bitterleaf Salad with Walnut Dressing given opposite.

2 pounds pumpkin, weighed with the skin and seeds
2 Tbs butter
salt and freshly ground black pepper

8 ounces firm goat cheese log or logs, cut into thin slices
½ cup finely grated fresh Parmesan cheese

Set the oven to 400°F.

Cut the skin from the pumpkin and remove the seeds and threads, then cut the flesh into even-sized pieces. Cook the pumpkin in boiling water to cover, or steam it until it is tender, then drain and mash it with the butter. (Keep the cooking water, which makes an excellent stock.) Season the pumpkin purée with salt and pepper and put half of it into a shallow gratin dish.

Cut the goat cheese into thin slices and put these on top of the pumpkin in the dish, then spoon the rest of the pumpkin on top. Sprinkle with the Parmesan cheese and bake for about 30 minutes, or until the gratin is hot and bubbling and the cheese on top is golden brown.

SERVES 4

BITTERLEAF SALAD WITH WALNUT DRESSING

Put 2 tablespoons light olive oil, 1 tablespoon walnut oil, 1 tablespoon red wine vinegar and salt and pepper into a salad bowl and stir. Wash 2 heads of Belgian endive, a radicchio and a small red curly leaf lettuce, separating the leaves. Shake them dry, then tear them into the bowl. Add snipped chives.

Just before you want to serve the salad, toss the leaves so that they all get coated in the dressing, and add about ¼-½ cup chopped walnuts.

BROILED RED BELL PEPPER AND EGGPLANT

Allow ½-1 red bell pepper and ½ medium-large (12-ounce) eggplant for each person. Quarter the bell peppers, place them shiny-side up on a broiler pan and broil at full heat until the skin has blistered and begun to char all over. Cover them with a plate and leave until they're cool enough to handle. Slip off the skins with a sharp knife and rinse the bell peppers to remove the seeds. Finally, slice the flesh.

Cut the eggplant into 2-inch slices. Brush a little olive oil on a broiler pan, put the eggplant slices on this (no need to salt them first) and brush the top surface with olive oil. Broil them until the tops are browned. You'll probably find that the bottoms are browned, too; if not, turn the slices over and do the other sides. The eggplants are done when they're browned on both sides and feel tender when pierced with a knife. Blot off any excess oil and serve them with the red bell pepper.

OPPOSITE: *Pumpkin and Goat Cheese Gratin*

LENTILS AND CILANTRO WITH YOGURT SAUCE

If you can't get fresh cilantro, use parsley – preferably flat-leaf if you can get it.

I use canned green lentils for this because they're so quick, although you could use dried ones if you preferred. If you do use dried lentils, you would need ½ cup; just boil them in plenty of water for 45-60 minutes, or until they are tender – there's no need to soak them first, although if you do it will make the cooking time a bit shorter. And if you cook extra, for another time, they'll freeze perfectly in a suitable container. Serve with the Broiled Red Bell Pepper and Eggplant dish on page 84 and a tossed green salad.

2 tsp olive oil
1 onion, peeled and
 sliced
2 tsp ground coriander
1¾ cups canned green
 lentils, drained
2 Tbs chopped fresh
 cilantro leaves

FOR THE SAUCE
1 small garlic clove,
 crushed
⅔ cup plain low-fat
 yogurt
salt and freshly ground
 black pepper

Heat the oil in a medium saucepan then put in the onion, cover and cook for 10 minutes, or until it is tender. Stir in the ground coriander and cook for a further 2 minutes. Add the drained lentils, stir gently, and cook for a few minutes until they're heated through. Then add the cilantro leaves.

Meanwhile, make a quick sauce by stirring the garlic into the yogurt and seasoning with salt and pepper. Serve the lentils and sauce garnished with the broiled bell pepper and eggplant slices.
SERVES 2

SPICY CHICK PEAS WITH YOGURT AND PAPRIKA SAUCE

This is very quick, cheap, healthy and easy. I like it just as it is, but for a more substantial meal you can add some good bread – focaccia or a Middle Eastern bread would be pleasant – or some cooked brown rice with some chopped herbs mixed into it.

3½ cups canned
 chick peas
6-8 plum tomatoes
8 sprigs of flat-leaf
 parsley
1 Tbs olive oil
1 tsp cumin seeds
salt and freshly ground
 black pepper

FOR THE SAUCE
⅔ cup plain
 low-fat yogurt
small garlic clove,
 crushed (optional)
½ tsp paprika pepper

First make the sauce: mix together the yogurt and garlic, if you're using this, season to taste and leave on one side.

Drain the chick peas; wash and slice the tomatoes, wash the flat-leaf parsley and remove the leaves from the stems. Heat the oil in a large saucepan and add the cumin. Fry it for about 1 minute, until the seeds start to pop, then put in the tomatoes and chick peas. Stir over the heat for 2-3 minutes, until everything is heated through, then add the parsley and season to taste.

Serve the mixture on warm plates, pour on some of the sauce, and sprinkle the sauce with paprika. Or you can serve the sauce separately in a bowl, with the paprika sprinkled on top.
SERVES 4

OPPOSITE: *Spicy Chick Peas with Yogurt and Paprika Sauce*

SPAGHETTI WITH SPICY TOMATO AND RED BELL PEPPER SAUCE

This quantity of sauce is right for two people or three at a pinch. If you're using whole wheat pasta, 3 ounces per person will probably be enough, as it's more filling; otherwise, allow 4 ounces per person.

6-8 ounces whole wheat or plain spaghetti	*1 onion, peeled and chopped*
olive oil	*1 red bell pepper*
salt and freshly ground black pepper	*1 garlic clove, crushed*
	1¼ cups canned tomatoes in juice
FOR THE SAUCE	*1 dried red chili, crumbled*
1 Tbs olive oil	

First get the sauce started. Heat the oil in a medium saucepan and put in the onion; cover and cook gently for a few minutes while you wash, seed and chop the red bell pepper. Add this to the pan, along with the garlic, and cook for a further 5 minutes with a lid on the pan. Put in the tomatoes, together with their juice, and the red chili. Mash the tomatoes a bit with a wooden spoon to make sure everything is well mixed, then cover and cook for about 15-20 minutes, or until all the vegetables are tender and the sauce is thick. Give the sauce a stir from time to time to make sure it isn't sticking.

Meanwhile, fill a large saucepan two-thirds full with water and heat it for the pasta. When the water is boiling, a few minutes before the sauce is ready, put the pasta into the water; give it a quick stir, let it come back to a boil and leave it to bubble away, uncovered, for about 8 minutes, or whatever it says on the package.

Drain the pasta, then tip it back into the warm pan and add a little olive oil and some salt and pepper. Serve immediately, with the sauce.
SERVES 2

OPPOSITE: *(left) Endive and Watercress Salad and (right) Spaghetti Squash with Gorgonzola, Cream and Walnuts*

SPAGHETTI SQUASH WITH GORGONZOLA, CREAM, AND WALNUTS

Almost any salad goes well with this – the Endive and Watercress Salad given below is a particular favorite.

2 pounds spaghetti squash	*salt and freshly ground black pepper*
2 Tbs butter	*½ cup roughly chopped walnuts*
⅔ cup heavy cream	
1 cup grated Gorgonzola cheese	*freshly grated Parmesan cheese*

Bring to a boil two large saucepans of water: each pan should be big enough to hold one of the spaghetti squash whole. Prick the squash in a few places, then put one in each saucepan, cover and boil for 30 minutes, or until the squash is tender when pierced with a skewer. Drain the squash and, holding them with a cloth, halve them and scoop out the 'spaghetti' into a hot saucepan. Add the butter, cream, Gorgonzola cheese and some salt and pepper to taste. Stir quickly over a gentle heat, just to distribute all the ingredients.

Scatter over the walnuts, sprinkle with Parmesan and serve at once, on warmed plates.
SERVES 4-6

ENDIVE AND WATERCRESS SALAD

Put 1 tablespoon red wine vinegar into a bowl with 3 tablespoons olive oil and some salt and a good grinding of pepper. Wash and dry 2 heads of Belgian endive, ½ curly endive and a bunch of watercress. Tear the endives into manageable pieces and put them into the bowl along with the watercress, on top of the dressing. Toss the salad just before you want to serve it.

I love those squashes which, when cooked, contain many strands, like spaghetti. You can cook them in many of the ways you'd cook spaghetti, but they're lighter, and, if you're food combining and not mixing starchy foods like pasta with proteins such as cheese, they're particularly useful as a pasta – replacement.

CABBAGE PARCELS WITH TOMATO SAUCE

As a variation, you could use large spinach or Swiss chard leaves instead of cabbage.

For this recipe you need cabbage leaves which are big enough to make into parcels, but tender. Young green cabbage is ideal, although you'll be left with the heart of the cabbage; shredded and mixed with mayonnaise, yogurt and lemon juice, it makes a good salad. The cabbage parcels can be served on their own and this quantity, I found, was greedily consumed by two people; under more restrained circumstances, they can be served with another vegetable like green beans, and maybe some baby new potatoes, and made to serve four.

1 green cabbage
2 Tbs olive oil
2 onions, peeled and chopped
1 garlic clove, crushed
1¾ cups canned tomatoes in juice
salt and freshly ground black pepper

2 cups small cultivated mushrooms
1½ cups grated Cheddar cheese
½ cup freshly grated Parmesan cheese

Set the oven to 400°F.

First, half-fill a large saucepan with water and bring to a boil; while it's heating up, remove and discard any very tough leaves from the cabbage, then carefully ease off any that seem reasonably large and tender, aiming for eight. When the water boils, put in the cabbage leaves, pushing them down below water level. Cover and cook for 5 minutes or so, until they are tender but not completely soggy. Drain them into a colander and refresh them under cold running water. Finally, spread them out on paper towels and blot them dry.

While the cabbage is cooking, heat the oil in another pan and add the onions; cover and cook gently for 5 minutes, then add the garlic and cook for a further 5 minutes. After this, put half the onion mixture into another pan and add the tomatoes and their juice, mashing them with a wooden spoon. Let them cook away for about 15 minutes until they form a thick sauce, then whizz them in a food processor and season with salt and pepper. Wash

and slice the mushrooms and add these to the pan containing the rest of the onion; fry for 3-4 minutes, until the mushrooms are tender, then remove from the heat and add the grated Cheddar cheese. Mix well, and put a bit of this mixture in the center of each cabbage leaf; fold over the sides, and roll each leaf up into a neat parcel. Put the parcels into a shallow ovenproof dish, pour the tomato sauce over and sprinkle the grated Parmesan over the top in a fairly thick layer. Bake for 25-30 minutes, until it's hot and bubbling, and the top is golden brown and crisp.

SERVES 2-4

MEXICAN CHILES RELLENOS

This recipe can be prepared ready for baking ahead of time, and the best accompaniment, I think, is a simple, plain salad.

8 small green bell peppers, each about 3 ounces
1½ cups grated vegetarian Cheddar cheese

FOR THE SAUCE
2 Tbs olive oil

2 onions, peeled and sliced
2-4 garlic cloves, crushed
3½ cups canned tomatoes
chili powder
salt and freshly ground black pepper

Set the oven to 400°F.

Broil the bell peppers at full heat until the skin has blistered and charred all over, turning the bell peppers around as necessary. Remove from the heat and leave until they're cool enough to handle.

While the bell peppers are broiling, make the sauce. Heat the oil in a large saucepan and put in the onions; cover and cook gently for 5 minutes, add the garlic, cover again, and cook for a further 5 minutes. Put in the tomatoes, together with their liquid, and a good pinch of chili powder, and cook, uncovered, for about 10 minutes, until much of the liquid has disappeared. Purée the mixture in a blender, then taste and add salt, pepper, and more chili powder, as necessary.

With your fingers and a sharp knife, slip the skins off the bell peppers. Make a slit down one side of each bell pepper and, with kitchen scissors, snip out the main section of seeds – don't worry if some are left, they won't hurt. Next, stuff each bell pepper with some of the grated cheese. Pour some of the tomato sauce into a shallow casserole, put the peppers on top, then pour the rest of the sauce over them. Bake them, uncovered, for about 20 minutes.

SERVES 4

ARTICHOKE BASES STUFFED WITH MUSHROOM MOUSSE

For this recipe you need some big artichokes, which are usually available in the early fall. Stuffed with a light mousse of mushrooms they're good either as an appetizer or, and I prefer them this way, as a main course. Some spinach, quickly steamed until it has wilted rather than cooked (see right), goes well with the stuffed artichokes.

8 globe artichokes	salt and freshly ground
lemon juice	black pepper
2 pounds mushrooms	½ cup pine nuts
4 Tbs butter	
2-3 garlic cloves,	FOR THE CHIVE AND
crushed	LEMON BUTTER
2 Tbs heavy cream	6 Tbs butter
2 Tbs chopped fresh	2 Tbs lemon juice
parsley, preferably	1 Tbs snipped chives
flat-leaf	

First prepare the artichokes by cutting off most of the leaves to reveal the choke, scraping this out, and trimming and tidying the remaining leaf-bases to form a neat shallow cup. Brush the cut surfaces

with some lemon juice to preserve their color, then cook them in a large panful of boiling water for 20-30 minutes, or until the bases are tender when pierced with a sharp knife. Put them upside down in a colander to drain. Meanwhile, wash the mushrooms, then chop them roughly. Melt the butter in a large saucepan, put in the garlic and mushrooms and cook, without a lid, for about 30 minutes, or until the mushrooms are tender and all their liquid has gone.

Set the oven to 400°F. When the mushrooms are done, put them into a food processor and whizz to a purée. Add the cream, a squeeze of lemon juice, the parsley and some salt and freshly ground black pepper to taste.

Pat the artichoke bases dry with paper towels as necessary and put them, cup-side up, in a lightly greased shallow casserole. Spoon the mushroom mixture into them and top each with a teaspoon of pine nuts. Bake them, uncovered, for about 15 minutes, or until they are heated through and the nuts are golden.

While they're cooking, make the chive and lemon butter: melt the butter in a small saucepan, add the lemon juice, chives and a little salt and pepper as necessary. Serve the artichokes on warmed plates, with a pool of the sauce.

SERVES 4

For wilted spinach you need 1–1½ pounds tender spinach leaves, without much in the way of stem, for four people. Put into ¼ inch of boiling water in a large saucepan, stirring for a few seconds until the leaves have wilted. (You may need to do several batches.) Transfer them to a warm dish, add salt, pepper, olive oil or butter.

MUSHROOMS

MUSHROOM 'CAVIAR'

As well as being good as an appetizer with some crisp Melba or plain toast, mushroom 'caviar' makes a good topping for canapés. Including some dried mushrooms in the mixture gives it extra flavor.

½ ounce (about ½ cup) dried morels or porcini mushrooms	*salt and freshly ground black pepper*
1 pound mushrooms	
1 garlic clove, peeled	**TO SERVE**
2-4 Tbs chopped fresh parsley	*a little sour cream*
2 Tbs butter	*paprika pepper*
squeeze of fresh lemon juice	*sprigs of flat-leaf parsley*
	crisp toast triangles

First prepare the dried mushrooms by putting them into a bowl and adding boiling water just to cover them. Leave them to soak for about an hour. Drain the mushrooms, straining the liquid through a fine strainer or a piece of cheesecloth to remove any sand. Reserve the liquid. If you have a food processor, put the dried mushrooms in that, along with the ordinary mushrooms, washed, the garlic and the parsley, and whizz until everything is finely chopped. Without a food processor, chop all these ingredients by hand; get them as fine as you can.

Heat the butter in a large saucepan and put in the chopped ingredients, stir, then cook uncovered for 15-20 minutes, or until any liquid which the mushrooms produce has boiled away. Pour in the reserved mushroom soaking liquid and a squeeze of lemon juice and cook for a few more minutes until the mixture is dry again. Remove from the heat and season.

Serve hot, warm or cold, on individual plates, with a heaping teaspoonful of sour cream, a sprinkling of paprika and a sprig of flat-leaf parsley on each. Accompany with crisp triangles of toast.
SERVES 4

WILD MUSHROOM DIP

If you've just got a few precious wild mushrooms, this dip makes the most of them, and the addition of some porcini intensifies the flavor.

¼ ounce (about ¼ cup) dried mushrooms, porcini or morels	*2 Tbs butter*
	1 cup farmer's cheese
1 cup wild mushrooms	*salt and freshly ground black pepper*

Put the dried mushrooms into a bowl and add boiling water just to cover them. Leave them to soak for an hour. Drain the mushrooms, straining the liquid through a fine strainer or a piece of cheesecloth, to remove any sand. Reserve the soaking liquid.

Wash the wild mushrooms, chop them with the dried porcini and cook them in the butter for 5 minutes, before adding the reserved soaking liquid. Let the mixture bubble away for 10 minutes or so until practically all the liquid has gone and the mushrooms are tender. Remove them from the heat.

When the mushrooms are cool, beat them into the farmer's cheese to make a creamy mixture, and season with salt and freshly ground black pepper. Serve with crudités or pita fingers.
SERVES 4

OPPOSITE: *(top) Mushroom 'Caviar' and (bottom) Oyster Mushroom and Porcini Timbale (page 94)*

OYSTER MUSHROOM AND PORCINI TIMBALE

Because oyster mushrooms are flat, I thought they would look interesting if I layered them into a loaf pan, then set them in place with a light custard. This timbale is the result and I think it makes a really attractive and unusual main dish, good served with a Red Wine Sauce and some seasonal vegetables like the Braised Celery on page 95.

¼ ounce (about ¼ cup) dried mushrooms, porcini or morels	1 garlic clove, crushed
	salt and freshly ground black pepper
1¼ pounds oyster mushrooms	2 eggs
4 Tbs butter	⅔ cup light cream

You can buy porcini in small packets. They're not cheap but they go a long way and the flavor is excellent.

Set the oven to 325°F. Line a small loaf pan with a piece of parchment paper to cover the base and extend up the short sides; grease the other sides. Put the dried mushrooms into a bowl and add boiling water just to cover them. Leave them to soak for about an hour. While they are soaking, prepare the oyster mushrooms by washing them then gently squeezing out the excess water and patting them dry.

Melt the butter in a large saucepan and add the oyster mushrooms. Let them cook for about 20 minutes, without a lid on the pan, until they are very tender and have absorbed their liquid. Drain the dried mushrooms, straining the liquid through a fine strainer or a piece of cheesecloth to remove any sand; chop the dried mushrooms finely. Add the chopped mushrooms and their liquid to the oyster mushrooms, along with the garlic, and cook for a further few minutes until they are again dry. Take them off the heat and season with salt and pepper.

Arrange the oyster mushrooms in the loaf pan in layers. Whisk together the eggs and cream, then pour this custard into the loaf pan, gently moving the oyster mushrooms with a knife and tipping the pan, to make sure that the custard seeps down between all the layers. Put the loaf pan in a roasting pan of boiling water and bake it for about 40 minutes, or until it is set and golden brown and a skewer inserted into the center comes out clean. Run a knife around the edges of the timbale to loosen it, then turn it out on to a warmed serving dish.

This timbale cuts well both hot and cold, but you need to use a sharp, serrated knife.

SERVES 6

TOMATO AND RED WINE SAUCE

1 onion, peeled and sliced	1¼ cups red wine
1 celery stalk, chopped	1¾ cups canned tomatoes
1 garlic clove, crushed	salt and freshly ground black pepper
1 Tbs olive oil	
sprig of fresh thyme	1 Tbs cold butter

Fry the onion, celery and garlic in the olive oil with the thyme for 10 minutes, browning them slightly, then add the wine and tomatoes. Bring to a boil, then let the sauce bubble away for about 5 minutes, to cook the tomatoes and thicken a bit. Purée the sauce in a blender, then pour it through a strainer into a saucepan. Season with salt and pepper.

Just before serving the sauce, bring it back to a boil then remove it from the heat and whisk in the butter, a little at a time, to make the sauce look glossy and thicken it a little more.

BRAISED CELERY

First trim off any roots from 2 heads of celery, then cut the stems down to about 6 inches from the base. Now take a vegetable parer and shave the outside stalks of the celery to remove any tough threads. Cut the celery down into quarters and wash them well under cold running water.

Heat 2 tablespoons olive oil in a large saucepan, add 1 teaspoon coriander seeds, a bay leaf, 6-8 peppercorns, and the pieces of celery. Turn the celery gently to coat it in the oil, add a sprinkling of salt, then pour in 2½ cups of water. Bring to a boil, cover and leave to cook gently for 1 hour, or until the celery is very tender. Remove the celery with a slotted spoon, put it into a shallow dish and keep it warm. Boil the remaining liquid hard to reduce it well and pour it over the celery. Sprinkle with some chopped parsley.

RAGOUT OF WILD MUSHROOMS

This is a dish to make when you've had a successful mushroom hunt, or feel like a no-expense-spared special fall meal. Alternatively, you can improvise by using a mixture of oyster, cultivated and shiitake mushrooms instead of the wild ones (see opposite). Some baby Brussels sprouts and early chestnuts, below, go well with this, to make a complete meal.

2¼ pounds wild	*lemon juice*
mushrooms	*salt and freshly ground*
6 Tbs butter	*black pepper*
3 garlic cloves, crushed	*chopped fresh parsley,*
4 Tbs heavy cream	*preferably flat-leaf*

Wash, trim and slice the mushrooms; pat them dry on paper towels. Melt the butter in a large saucepan and put in the mushrooms and garlic. Cook over a moderate heat, uncovered, until they are tender and any liquid that they make has bubbled away. The time varies according to the type of mushroom; it can be as little as 5 minutes, or as long as 20, but if you test the mushrooms with a sharp knife you'll be able to tell when they're tender.

Add the cream, a squeeze of lemon juice and some salt and pepper to season. Get the mixture really hot, sprinkle with parsley then serve at once.
SERVES 4

BABY SPROUTS AND EARLY CHESTNUTS

You'll need 1-1½ pounds Brussels sprouts for four people and 8-12 ounces chestnuts, weighed before peeling. Really baby sprouts can be trimmed and cooked whole, but if they are larger, I think they're better if you cut them in half. The chestnuts need to be prepared in advance. The easiest way to peel them is to put them on a board on their flat side and make a sharp cut from top to bottom. Put them into boiling water, a few at a time, and boil for 3-5 minutes, or until the cut opens. Then take them out and peel off the skins. Once they're peeled, they need to be cooked in fresh water for about 15 minutes, or until they're tender.

Cook the sprouts in ½ inch of fast-boiling water with a lid on the pan for 3-5 minutes, or until they're just done. Drain them (save the water as it makes good stock), add the hot cooked chestnuts with a little butter, and season with salt and freshly ground black pepper.

By wild mushrooms, I mean ceps (called porcini in Italy) or chanterelles (or morels in the spring) if you're lucky enough to get them; or oyster mushrooms or shiitake which are increasingly available from vegetable stores and supermarkets.

PERFECT DESSERTS

APPLE AND BLACKBERRY LAYER

For this light dessert I like to use the sweetest apples and blackberries I can find, because the sweeter they are, the less additional sugar you need. You could use cooking apples if you prefer, sweetened with sugar or honey; and for a less rich cream, you could use half heavy cream and half plain yogurt.

2¼ pounds sweet
  apples
sugar, honey or
  no-added-sugar
  apricot preserves

1 pound blackberries
1¼ cups heavy cream
¼ cup toasted slivered
  almonds

Peel, core and slice the apples, then put them into a heavy-based saucepan with 2 tablespoons of water. Cover and cook over a gentle heat for 10-15 minutes or until they have collapsed to a purée. Watch that they don't stick toward the end of the cooking time. Remove from the heat, taste, and add a little sugar, honey or no-added-sugar apricot preserves to sweeten as necessary, then leave to get cold.

Wash the blackberries, put them into a saucepan without any water and cook them over a gentle heat for a few minutes until the juices run. Remove from the heat and sweeten as necessary, then leave until cold. (If they release a lot of juice, strain the fruit from the liquid with a slotted spoon.)

To assemble the dessert, first whip the cream until it forms soft peaks. Put a layer of blackberry mixture into a glass bowl, using about half the mixture; then put half the apples in an even layer on top, and spread half the cream over them. Repeat the layers, ending with a layer of cream, and keeping a few berries in reserve to decorate the top of the dessert. Chill until required – it will keep overnight, if covered with plastic wrap and stored in the fridge. Sprinkle the toasted slivered almonds and reserved berries on top just before serving.
SERVES 4-6

SPICED PEAR COMPOTE WITH ORANGE CREAM

Although this may not look amazing, being rather low-key in its coloring, it tastes good, especially if you serve it with the orange cream.

2 pounds hard pears
3 cloves
½ cinnamon stick
¼ cup dark brown
  sugar

FOR THE ORANGE
CREAM

1 orange
⅔ cup thick, creamy
  yogurt or heavy
  cream

Cut the pears into quarters, remove the peel and cores and slice the flesh fairly thinly. Put the slices into a large saucepan with the cloves, cinnamon stick, sugar and enough water to cover: I used 2½ cups. Bring to a boil, then let them simmer until the pears are very tender and the liquid is reduced to a syrupy glaze. Remove from the heat and leave to cool – this compôte is good served either warm or cold.

To make the orange cream, first remove a few long strands of peel with an orange zester for decoration, then grate enough peel to produce about a teaspoonful: finally, squeeze the orange. Add the grated peel to the yogurt or cream, along with 1-2 tablespoons of the juice, or enough to give a good flavor. If you're using cream, whisk it gently until it falls in soft peaks.

Serve the spiced pear compôte in individual bowls, either with a spoonful of cream and some slivers of orange peel on top, which I think is prettiest; or, if not everyone wants cream, serve this in a separate small bowl, decorated with the orange peel slivers.
SERVES 4

OPPOSITE: *Apple and Blackberry Layer*

PEAR AND ALMOND TART

This is an unusual tart in which the base is made of ground almonds instead of pastry, and maple syrup is used for sweetening. Some lightly whipped cream with a dash of amaretto or poire william eau de vie would be the final touch for a special occasion.

1½ pounds sweet pears	1 tsp baking powder
6 Tbs maple syrup	1 Tbs maple syrup
1 vanilla bean	2 Tbs butter
	few drops real almond extract (optional)

FOR THE TART SHELL

1¾ cups ground
  almonds

Set the oven to 350°F. Cut the pears into quarters and remove the peel and cores, then cut the flesh into thin slices. Put them into a heavy-based saucepan with the maple syrup and the vanilla bean and cook gently, uncovered, for about 10 minutes. The pears should be tender and almost transparent, and bathed in a glossy glaze after this time. Allow to cool.

Meanwhile, make the tart shell: mix together, by hand or in a food processor, the ground almonds, baking powder, maple syrup, butter and, if you wish to intensify the almond flavor, a few drops of real almond extract. Press the somewhat sticky dough into an 8-inch metal tart pan, pushing the mixture up the sides but being careful not to make it too thick. Prick the dough all over and bake for 10 minutes, until it is crisp and golden brown. Remove from the oven and leave to cool.

Not more than an hour or so before serving the tart, arrange the pear slices on top of the pastry, removing the vanilla bean (rinse, dry and use again). Pour any glossy liquid from the pan over the pears; if it is watery rather than glossy, boil it up for a few minutes to reduce it before using.

SERVES 6

OPPOSITE: *Pear and Almond Tart*

FIGS WITH MASCARPONE

If you can get some perfect figs, this is a luscious way to eat them. I think they need a light red-fruit coulis to go with them; one made from raspberries is best if you can get them, otherwise you could use sweet ripe red plums.

raspberry coulis (see page 63)	8 sweet ripe figs
	½ cup mascarpone

First, make the coulis, which can be done well in advance – then chill it in the fridge.

Just before you want to serve the dessert, pour a small pool of raspberry coulis on to four plates. Stand the figs on a board with their stalk uppermost, and cut them down, through the stalk, into sixths or eighths, keeping them attached at the base. Put a couple of figs on each plate and open out the cut sections like the petals of a flower. Spoon a little mascarpone into the center of each 'flower', and trickle a little of the raspberry coulis on top.

SERVES 4

FALL MENUS

MENU

A HARVEST SUPPER PARTY FOR EIGHT

Pumpkin Soup

Eggplant, Tomato and Mozzarella Bake
Roasted Bell Peppers Stuffed with Fennel
Fall Green Salad with Toasted Hazelnuts

Fruit Salad with
Scented Geranium Cream
Apple Almond Cake

COUNTDOWN

Up to 1 day before:
Make the Pumpkin Soup, cover and keep in the
fridge. Make the Apple Almond Cake and
the filling, but don't assemble. Make the Eggplant,
Tomato and Mozzarella Bake ready for baking.

2-3 hours before:
Make the Fruit Salad, cover; wash the
salad and keep in the fridge.

1½ hours before:
Set the oven to 350°F. Prepare the Bell Peppers and
put them into the oven to cook.
30-40 minutes before you want to seve the meal, move
the bell peppers to the coolest part of the oven
and turn up the heat to 425°F. Put the
Eggplant Bake into the oven. Cover the bell peppers
with foil if they start to brown too much. Split and fill
the cake; make the Geranium Cream;
gently reheat the soup; finish making the salad.

PUMPKIN SOUP

Pumpkin makes a beautiful soup, golden and creamy,
with a delicate flavor – and it couldn't be easier to
prepare.

3 pounds pumpkin,
weighed with skin
and seeds
4 Tbs butter
1 large onion, peeled
and chopped
2 garlic cloves, crushed
2 Tbs light cream

salt and freshly ground
black pepper
fresh lemon juice

TO GARNISH
fresh chives
flat-leaf parsley

Cut the skin from the pumpkin and remove the
seeds and threads, then cut the flesh into even-
sized pieces. Heat the butter in a large saucepan
and put in the onion. Cook, covered, for 5 minutes,
until it is beginning to soften, then add the garlic
and pumpkin. Stir, then cover the pan again and
cook for a further 5-10 minutes. Add 4½ pints water,
bring to a boil, then half-cover the pan and let the
soup simmer for 30 minutes, or until the pumpkin
is very tender.

Purée the soup thoroughly in a blender, then
pour it back into the saucepan, stir in the cream,
and season with salt, pepper and a little squeeze of
lemon juice to lift the flavor, if necessary.

Reheat and pour into warmed bowls, then snip
some chives and parsley over each bowl.

OPPOSITE: *Dishes from A Harvest Supper Party*
for Eight

EGGPLANT, TOMATO AND MOZZARELLA BAKE

This warming casserole is as delicious to eat as it is easy to make; make sure you've got lots of crusty bread handy to mop up the juices.

2 small-medium eggplants, 1 pound in all	glass of red wine (optional)
salt	salt and freshly ground black pepper
1 large onion	8 ounces mozzarella cheese (packed in water)
olive oil	
2 garlic cloves	½ cup freshly grated Parmesan cheese
3½ cups canned plum tomatoes	
1 tsp dried oregano	

Any of the following would be good to drink with this supper: hard cider, an aromatic dry white wine such as Gewurztraminer, a light dry wine such as Muscadet, or a White Burgundy.

Set the oven to 425°F. Cut the eggplants into ¼-inch slices, discarding the stalk. Layer the slices into a colander, sprinkling each layer with salt. Put a plate and a weight on top of the eggplant and leave to drain for 10-30 minutes, depending on how rushed you are.

Meanwhile, make a rich tomato sauce. Peel and chop the onion then fry it in 1-2 tablespoons of olive oil for 5 minutes. Peel and crush the garlic and add to the pan, along with the tomatoes and their liquid, the oregano and the red wine if you're using it. Break up the tomatoes a bit with a wooden spoon, then leave the mixture to cook, uncovered, for about 15-20 minutes, or until the liquid has reduced considerably, leaving a thick, purée-like mixture. Stir from time to time. Season the sauce with salt and pepper.

Rinse the eggplants under cold water and pat the slices dry with a clean cloth or paper towels. Heat 2 tablespoons of olive oil in a skillet and fry the eggplant slices in a single layer – you'll need to do several batches. After a minute or two turn the slices over, so that they get cooked and lightly browned on both sides. Lift them out on to a plate or cookie sheet lined with paper towels and fry the next batch. Cut the mozzarella cheese into slices about ¼ inch thick.

To assemble the dish, put a layer of half the eggplant slices into a large, shallow casserole. Pour half the sauce on top and then lay the cheese slices on top of that. Cover with the remaining eggplant slices and the rest of the sauce, then sprinkle the Parmesan cheese on top. Bake for 30-40 minutes, or until the topping has turned golden brown and the mixture is bubbling. Serve at once.

ROASTED BELL PEPPERS STUFFED WITH FENNEL

This is a slight adaptation of one of Delia Smith's recipes which I like very much. It can be served hot or cold as a first course or accompanying vegetable, and I also like it as a light main course with other vegetables. The bell peppers need to be good medium-sized ones, rather square in shape; and the fennel needs to be fairly small so that when cut into eighths two pieces will fit inside the peppers side by side.

2 fennel bulbs	salt and freshly ground black pepper
4 red bell peppers	
1¾ cups canned tomatoes in juice	1 tbs coriander seeds
	5 tbs olive oil

Set the oven to 350°F. Bring 1 inch of water to a boil in a medium saucepan. Cut the leafy tops off the fennel, trim the root ends and remove a layer of the white part if it looks as if it's tough. Cut the fennel down into quarters, then eighths, keeping them joined at the base. Cook the fennel in the water, with a lid on the pan, for 5-7 minutes, or until it's tender, then drain it. (Keep the water – it makes marvellous stock.)

Halve the bell peppers, cutting right down through the stalks, remove the seeds and trim the white part inside to make a good cavity. Arrange the peppers in a roasting pan or shallow casserole. Chop the tomatoes and divide the mixture between the bell peppers, adding a little of the juice as necessary. Season with salt and freshly ground black pepper, then place two pieces of fennel side by side inside the bell peppers and on top of the tomato, with the root-end toward the stem end of the fennel; push them down neatly to fit and season again. Crush the coriander seeds in a pestle with a mortar or with the end of a rolling pin or wooden spoon, and sprinkle them over the top of the fennel. Finally, pour some olive oil over the top of each bell pepper half.

Bake the bell peppers, uncovered, for about 1 hour, or until they are very tender and beginning to brown. Serve hot or cold.

FALL GREEN SALAD WITH TOASTED HAZELNUTS

When you're working out quantities for a party, one of the strange laws of life is that the more people present, the less salad they'll eat. So, under normal circumstances, I'd expect this salad to serve four salad-lovers, but for a harvest supper with more people (and lots of other food), it will be enough for about eight.

1 tbs hazelnut oil, if available
2 tbs olive oil or 3 tbs if you're not using hazelnut oil
1 tbs wine vinegar
salt and freshly ground black pepper
2-4 artichoke hearts, cooked, cooled and sliced, or 1 avocado, peeled and sliced

½ curly endive
bunch of watercress (about 3 cups trimmed watercress)
1 celery heart
2 tbs snipped fresh chives
½ cup skinned hazelnuts, toasted under the broiler

Mix the dressing straight into a salad bowl: put in the hazelnut oil, if you're using it, the olive oil, wine vinegar and some salt and freshly ground black pepper and mix together. Add the artichoke hearts

or avocado and mix gently. Wash the curly endive and watercress, shake them dry, then put them into the bowl, tearing large pieces as necessary. Slice the celery heart finely, and add that to the bowl, too, along with the chives.

Just before you want to serve the salad, turn it gently so that all the leaves get lightly coated with the dressing, and add the chopped nuts.

FRUIT SALAD WITH SCENTED GERANIUM CREAM

Start making the geranium sugar a few days before you want to serve this dessert, and the cream the night before, to give the flavor a chance to develop.

FOR THE FRUIT SALAD
1 pound blueberries or blackberries
2 cups cherry and red currant sugar-free preserves
5 sweet apples
5 sweet pears
5 sweet figs

FOR THE CREAM
1¼ cups heavy cream
2-3 scented geranium leaves, lemon or rose scent not mint
sugar
extra geranium leaves to decorate

The geranium cream is made by sweetening the heavy cream with sugar which has been flavored with geranium. To make this sugar, bury several scented geranium leaves in a small jar of sugar and leave for 3-4 days or longer (like making vanilla sugar).

To make the fruit salad, wash the blueberries or blackberries and take out any damaged ones or stems. Put them into a heavy-based saucepan with the sugar-free preserves and heat gently until the preserves have melted and the fruit juices begin to run. Pour the mixture into a bowl and leave on one side to cool down. Meanwhile, peel, core, and thinly slice the apples and pears; wash and slice the figs. Add all these to the fruit mixture in the bowl

The sweetening I love to use for the fruit salad is no-added-sugar cherry and red currant spread. This is delicate in flavor, whereas some of the other no-added-sugar spreads available are rather powerful.

and stir gently so that everything is distributed. Cover and leave until required.

Just before you want to serve the fruit salad, make the geranium cream. Whisk the cream until it makes soft peaks, then gently stir in a little of the geranium-scented sugar to flavor and sweeten it. Transfer the cream to a serving bowl. Garnish with a few scented geranium leaves and serve with the fruit salad.

APPLE ALMOND CAKE

This cake consists of layers of light, quick-to-make almond-flavored sponge cake sandwiched together with a thick purée of apples with amaretto liqueur. You can make both the sponge cake and the apple purée a day or two in advance, but do not fill the cake until shortly before you want to eat it if you do. For a really luscious, richer variation, you could spread each of the layers with whipped cream as well as apple purée.

FOR THE ALMOND SPONGE CAKE

¾ *cup soft butter*
¾ *cup sugar*
3 eggs
½ *cup ground almonds*
1 tsp almond extract
1½ cups self-rising flour
1½ tsp baking powder
¼ *cup slivered almonds*

FOR THE APPLE FILLING

2¼ pounds sweet apples, peeled and sliced
3 Tbs amaretto liqueur (optional)
no-added-sugar apricot preserves, honey or sugar to taste

Set the oven to 325°F. Line a deep 8-inch round cake pan with parchment paper. To make the cake, put the butter, sugar, eggs, ground almonds and almond extract into a bowl, or the bowl of a mixer or food processor, then sift in the flour and baking powder. Whisk or process for a minute or two until

the mixture is smooth and glossy, then add 3 tablespoons of water to make a mixture which is soft enough to drop reluctantly off a spoon. Spoon the mixture into the prepared pan, level the top, sprinkle with the slivered almonds and bake for 1-1¼ hours, until a wooden toothpick inserted into the center comes out clean. Cool for 10 minutes in the pan, then transfer to a wire rack. Remove the paper when the cake is cold.

To make the filling, put the apples into a heavy-based saucepan with 2 tablespoons of water. Cover and cook over a gentle heat for 10-15 minutes or until they have collapsed to a thick purée, stirring the mixture often to prevent it from sticking. Remove from the heat and allow to cool completely, then add the amaretto, if you're using it, and some no-added-sugar preserves, honey or sugar to taste.

Assemble the cake by cutting it across twice, to make three layers. Put the bottom layer on a plate and spread it with half the apple mixture, then put the next piece of sponge cake on top and press down. Spread with the rest of the apple purée and place the final layer, with the almonds in it, on top.

OPPOSITE: *Desserts from A Harvest Supper Party for Eight*

MENU

A HALLOWEEN PARTY FOR TEN TO TWELVE

Mexican Beanfeast with Tomato, Red Bell Pepper and Avocado Salsas

Pumpkin, Okra and Baby Corn Casserole

Maple Ice Cream Chocolate Pecan Brownies

Party Cider Cup

MEXICAN BEANFEAST

3 Tbs olive oil
1 Tbs cumin seeds
1 pound onions, peeled and sliced
1 garlic clove, crushed
1¾ cups canned pinto beans
1¾ cups canned red kidney beans
1¾ cups canned cannellini beans
1¾ cups canned black-eyed peas
chopped cilantro to garnish

Heat the oil in a large saucepan, then fry the cumin seeds for 30 seconds. Put in the onions and garlic and cook gently for 10 minutes, with a lid on the pan. Drain the beans, reserving the liquid. Add them to the saucepan, stirring very gently over a low heat to mix them all together, and heat them through without mashing them. Add a little of the reserved liquid if they are in danger of sticking.

Sprinkle with the chopped cilantro and serve with Tomato, Red Bell Pepper and Avocado Salsas, taco chips and a spoonful of sour cream.

COUNTDOWN

Up to 1 week ahead:
Make the Maple Ice Cream.

The day before:
Make the Chocolate Brownies.

Several hours in advance:
Make the Mexican Beanfeast, the Pumpkin, Okra and Baby Corn Casserole and the Tomato and Red Bell Pepper Salsas.

1 hour in advance:
Make the Avocado Salsa. Gently re-heat the Mexican Beanfeast and the Pumpkin, Okra and Baby Corn Casserole. Remove the Ice Cream from the freezer 30 minutes or so before you want to serve it.

TOMATO SALSA

1½-2 pounds ripe tomatoes
juice of 1 lemon
4 Tbs chopped fresh cilantro leaves
salt and freshly ground black pepper

Peel the tomatoes by covering them with boiling water, leaving for 60 seconds, then draining and slipping off the skins with a sharp knife. Chop the tomatoes coarsely, discarding any tough bits of stem, and put them into a bowl with the lemon juice, chopped cilantro and salt and pepper to taste. Serve in a bowl, to accompany the beanfeast.

OPPOSITE: *A Halloween Party for Ten to Twelve*

RED BELL PEPPER SALSA

3 large red bell peppers *salt and freshly ground*
3 green chilies *black pepper*
juice of 1 lemon

Cut the red bell peppers into quarters, then put them shiny-side up on a broiler pan, together with the chilies which can remain whole, and broil at full heat until the skin has blistered and begun to char. Move them halfway through broiling so that all the skin gets done, then cover them with a plate to keep in the steam. Leave until they're cool enough to handle, slip off the skins and rinse the bell peppers to remove the seeds. Skin the chilies, too, then halve them and rinse away the seeds.

Put the pieces of bell pepper and chili into a blender with the lemon juice and some salt and pepper and whizz to a purée. Check the seasoning, and serve in a small bowl.

AVOCADO SALSA

1 lime *salt and freshly ground*
2 avocados *black pepper*
1 green chili *paprika pepper*
1 garlic clove, crushed
  (optional)

Scrub the lime then, using a vegetable parer, peel off a few pieces of rind and snip or cut them into shreds to make about a tablespoonful. Squeeze the juice from the lime and put it into a bowl. Remove the peel and pits from the avocados, cut into rough chunks and put into the bowl with the lime juice. Halve, seed and finely slice the chili, being careful not to get the juice near your face or eyes (wash your hands afterwards), and add to the avocado, along with the garlic if you're using it, and the shreds of lime.

Mash all the ingredients together with a fork, to produce a mixture which is creamy without being too smooth. Season with salt and freshly ground black pepper. Spoon the mixture into a small bowl and garnish with a sprinkling of paprika.

SPICED PUMPKIN, OKRA AND BABY CORN CASSEROLE

2¼ pounds pumpkin, *1 cinnamon stick*
  weighed with skin *8-12 ounces okra*
  and seeds *8 ounces baby corn*
4 Tbs butter *1¼ cups canned*
2 Tbs olive oil *tomatoes in juice*
2 large onions, peeled *salt and freshly ground*
  and chopped *black pepper*
2 garlic cloves, crushed

Remove the peel, seeds and threads from the pumpkin and cut the flesh into fairly thin slices. Heat the butter and oil in a large saucepan and put in the onions; cover and cook for 5 minutes, then add the garlic, pumpkin and cinnamon stick, broken in two. Stir well, then cover again and cook for a further 10 minutes.

Wash and trim the okra and baby corn, then either cut them into ½-inch lengths or leave them whole, whichever you prefer, and add them to the pan. Chop the tomatoes and add these, too, along with their juice. Season with some salt and pepper, cover and leave the casserole to cook for 20 minutes, or until the vegetables are all tender.

Check the seasoning and transfer the mixture to a warmed casserole.

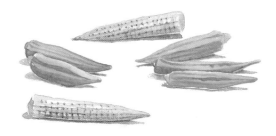

Accompany this menu with either the party cider cup or a medium-bodied French red wine such as Côtes du Rhône (domaine bottled).

MAPLE ICE CREAM

You don't have to stir this ice cream as it freezes in order to produce a smooth, velvety texture.

3 egg yolks	**1¼ cups heavy**
⅓ cup maple	**cream**
syrup	

Put the egg yolks into a bowl and whisk until they are pale and thick, preferably using an electric mixer. Put the maple syrup into a small saucepan and boil for 2-3 minutes, until the syrup reaches 225°F on a candy thermometer or a drop of it will form a thread when pulled between your finger and thumb. Remove from the heat immediately and pour the syrup on to the egg yolks while you whisk them. Continue to whisk for 2-3 minutes, until the mixture is cool and very thick and creamy. Whip the cream until it holds its shape, then fold it into the egg yolk mixture.

Pour the mixture into a plastic container and freeze until firm. Remove from the freezer about 15 minutes before you want to serve the ice cream to allow it to soften up a little, although it shouldn't get rock-solid in any case.

CHOCOLATE PECAN BROWNIES

Brownies always make a popular treat and are good to serve either as a cake or as a dessert. You can vary the nuts in these: skinned hazelnuts, brazil nuts or walnuts are also good.

10 ounces bittersweet	**2 tsp vanilla extract**
chocolate, not too	**¼ cup dark brown**
bitter, at least 50%	**sugar**
cocoa solids	**½ tsp baking powder**
½ cup butter or	**1 cup roughly chopped**
margarine	**pecans**
4 eggs	

Set the oven to 350°F. Line an 8-inch square cake pan with a piece of greased parchment paper. Break the chocolate into pieces, put it into a saucepan with the butter or margarine, and melt gently.

Meanwhile, put the eggs into a large bowl with the vanilla extract and the sugar and whisk at high speed in a mixer or with an electric hand beater for about 5 minutes, until they are very thick and pale. Whisk in the melted chocolate mixture and stir in the baking powder and the pecans. (There's no flour in this recipe, that's intentional!) Pour the mixture into the cake pan, easing it gently into the corners. Bake for 40 minutes. Cool in the pan, then cut into squares.

PARTY CIDER CUP

You can really make this cider cup to taste, adding more or less soda water and brandy as you prefer. It should be refreshing rather than too alcoholic and is a good thirst-quenching drink.

1 lemon	**½ cup brandy**
2-inch piece of	**2 quarts hard cider,**
cucumber	**apple cider or apple**
1 red-skinned apple	**juice**
6-8 sprigs of fresh	**5 cups soda water**
mint	**ice cubes**

Slice the lemon and cucumber finely; wash the apple and cut it into chunky pieces about the size of a cherry. Bruise the mint by crushing it a bit with a rolling pin. Put all these ingredients into a bowl or very large jug (or divide the mixture between two), add the brandy, then cover and leave until just before the party.

When you're ready to serve the cup, add the cider and soda water to the bowl or jug(s), stir, add the ice cubes and serve at once

Look out for real maple syrup, not 'maple-flavored' syrup.

WINTER

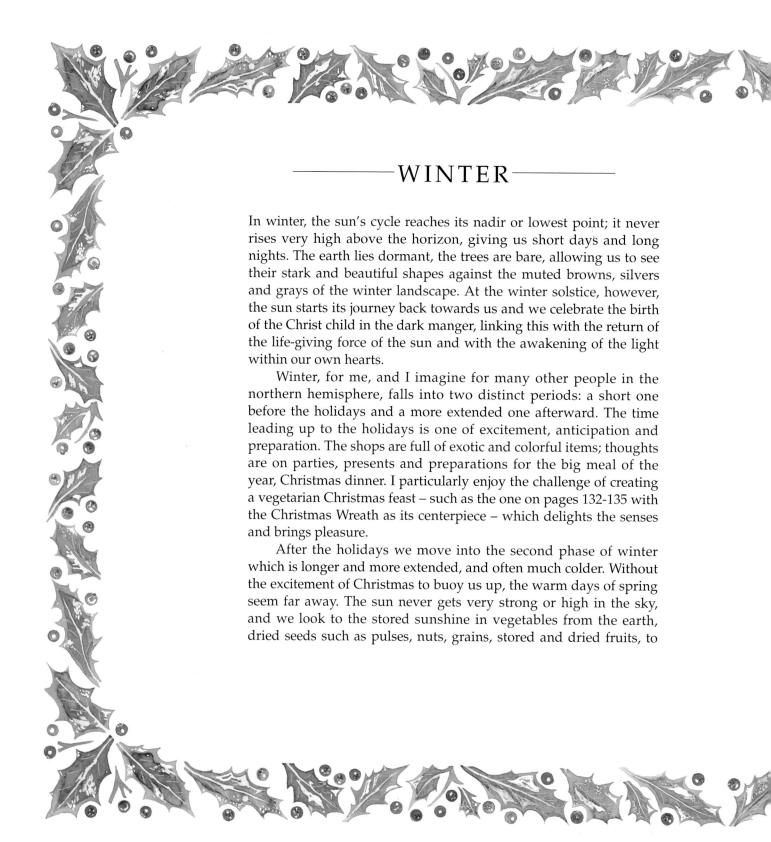

WINTER

In winter, the sun's cycle reaches its nadir or lowest point; it never rises very high above the horizon, giving us short days and long nights. The earth lies dormant, the trees are bare, allowing us to see their stark and beautiful shapes against the muted browns, silvers and grays of the winter landscape. At the winter solstice, however, the sun starts its journey back towards us and we celebrate the birth of the Christ child in the dark manger, linking this with the return of the life-giving force of the sun and with the awakening of the light within our own hearts.

Winter, for me, and I imagine for many other people in the northern hemisphere, falls into two distinct periods: a short one before the holidays and a more extended one afterward. The time leading up to the holidays is one of excitement, anticipation and preparation. The shops are full of exotic and colorful items; thoughts are on parties, presents and preparations for the big meal of the year, Christmas dinner. I particularly enjoy the challenge of creating a vegetarian Christmas feast – such as the one on pages 132-135 with the Christmas Wreath as its centerpiece – which delights the senses and brings pleasure.

After the holidays we move into the second phase of winter which is longer and more extended, and often much colder. Without the excitement of Christmas to buoy us up, the warm days of spring seem far away. The sun never gets very strong or high in the sky, and we look to the stored sunshine in vegetables from the earth, dried seeds such as pulses, nuts, grains, stored and dried fruits, to

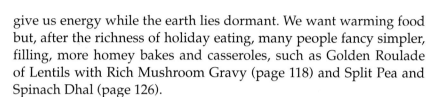

give us energy while the earth lies dormant. We want warming food but, after the richness of holiday eating, many people fancy simpler, filling, more homey bakes and casseroles, such as Golden Roulade of Lentils with Rich Mushroom Gravy (page 118) and Split Pea and Spinach Dhal (page 126).

Conversely, this is also a time when many people think about dieting and losing weight, an aspect of late-twentieth century living which goes totally against the rhythm of the seasons, when all the foods available suggest that this is a time when nature is encouraging us to gain a pound or two as protection against the cold. Constant worry about weight and the misery of being perpetually either on a diet or feeling one ought to be, is one of the sicknesses, I believe, of modern life in the affluent half of the world.

I used to be on this dieting switch-back – and being a cookery writer doesn't help. But I have found that, for me, the answer lies in compatible eating. That is, put simply, not mixing concentrated protein foods – eggs, cheese, dairy produce (and, for meat-eaters, meat, fish and poultry) – with concentrated carbohydrates or starches – bread, potatoes, pasta, flour, rice – at the same meal. Vegetables (except for potatoes, sweet potatoes and corn) go with everything. Food combining is really a subject in itself, perhaps for a future book, but I have given a brief explanation on page 5. Many of the recipes in this book are compatible, and these are listed in a separate index at the end of the book. I've found that by eating compatible foods, yet at the same time having a wide range of possibilities open to me, there's no feeling of being 'on a diet' or of having to count calories; I simply do not get the cravings for certain foods – especially the sweet ones and 'fattening' ones – that I used to.

SATISFYING SOUPS

WHITE WINTER SOUP WITH SUN-DRIED TOMATO PUREE

For a vegan version of white winter soup, replace the cream with a non-dairy cream, which you can buy at health food stores.

The sunshine flavor of sun-dried tomatoes turns this simple soup into a winter treat. Puréed sun-dried tomato is available in jars, otherwise sun-dried tomatoes in oil, puréed in a blender, are similar.

8 ounces celery root
8 ounces turnips
8 ounces leeks, white
   part only
1 Tbs light olive oil
sprig of fresh thyme

4 Tbs light cream
salt and freshly ground
   black pepper
4 tsp sun-dried tomato
   purée

Peel the celery root and turnips and cut them into even-sized pieces; trim, wash and slice the leeks. Heat the oil in a large saucepan and put in the vegetables and the thyme. Cook the vegetables, with a lid on the pan, for about 10 minutes, then add 3¾ cups of water. Bring to a boil, turn down the heat and leave the soup to simmer for about 30 minutes, or until the vegetables are very tender.

Remove the thyme, purée a ladleful of the soup in a blender with the cream, then add this to the rest of the soup. Season the soup with salt and pepper, reheat gently, and serve into warmed bowls. Top each with a swirl of sun-dried tomato purée.
SERVES 4

STILTON SOUP

If you haven't any good home-made stock (which doesn't have to be made specially if you make a habit of saving the water in which vegetables are cooked, especially tasty ones like celery root), it's much better to use water than a bouillon cube or powder. The celery, leeks and Stilton in this soup give it a good flavor in any case.

8 ounces outside celery
   stalks
8 ounces leeks
3¾ cups good
   vegetable stock or
   water
4 ounces Stilton
   cheese

salt and freshly ground
   black pepper
squeeze of lemon juice
1-2 Tbs cream
   (optional)
snipped chives or
   parsley to garnish

Scrub the celery and run a vegetable parer down each stalk to remove any stringy bits; trim and clean the leeks. Chop the celery and leeks and put them into a large saucepan along with the stock or water; cover, bring to a boil and leave to simmer gently for 1 hour, or until the vegetables are very tender.

Put the soup into a food processor and crumble in the cheese, in rough chunks. Whizz to a purée, then pour the mixture back into the saucepan through a strainer, pressing through any lumps of cheese. Season with salt and pepper; add a squeeze of fresh lemon juice to sharpen the flavor slightly if necessary, and stir in the cream if you're using this. Reheat gently, without boiling.

Top each bowlful with some chives or parsley.
SERVES 4

OPPOSITE: *White Winter Soup with Sun-dried Tomato Purée*

CREAM OF CELERY SOUP

Apart from tasting good, this soup is an excellent way of using the tough outer stalks of celery which always get left and tend to lurk in the back of the fridge waiting to be thrown out.

2 Tbs olive oil	*3¾ cups vegetable*
2 onions, peeled and	*stock or water*
chopped	*4 Tbs cream*
outside stalks of 1	*salt and freshly ground*
head of celery, about	*black pepper*
1 pound in all	

Heat the oil in a large saucepan and add the onions. Cover and cook over a gentle heat for 10 minutes, until the onions are soft but not browned.

Meanwhile, scrub the celery and run a vegetable parer down each stalk to remove any stringy bits. Chop the celery and add it to the onions, stir, cover, and cook for another 5 minutes. Add the stock or water, bring to a boil and leave the soup to cook gently for 1 hour, or until the celery is very tender.

Purée the soup in a blender and pour it through a strainer back into the saucepan to remove any remaining tough bits of celery. Stir in the cream and salt and pepper to taste and serve hot.
SERVES 4

MIDDLE EASTERN LENTIL SOUP

For a change, the lentil soup can be made with green lentils instead of split red ones.

1 cup split red lentils	*1 Tbs olive oil*
2 onions, peeled and	*2 tsp ground coriander*
chopped	*juice of ½ lemon*
2 celery stalks	*salt and freshly ground*
1 garlic clove, crushed	*black pepper*
1 tsp ground cumin	

This is a quick and simple lentil soup with a topping of onion fried with ground coriander to make it crisp and spicy. Put the lentils into a large saucepan with half the onions and 4 cups of water (or real vegetable stock if you have it). Run a vegetable parer down the celery to remove any stringy bits, then chop the celery and add to the pan, along with the garlic and cumin. Bring to a boil, then let the soup simmer gently for about 1 hour, until the celery and lentils are very tender.

While the soup is cooking, fry the rest of the onion in the oil with the coriander for about 10 minutes, or until it is tender but lightly browned and crisp. Purée the soup in a blender, add the lemon juice, season with salt and pepper, then stir in the fried onion and coriander. Serve at once.
SERVES 4

GOLDEN ONION SOUP WITH CHEESE TOPPING

2 Tbs butter	*7½ cups vegetable*
1 Tbs oil	*stock*
2 pounds onions,	*salt and freshly ground*
peeled and thinly	*black pepper*
sliced	*lemon juice*
2 garlic cloves, crushed	*1 cup grated*
	Gruyère cheese

Heat the butter and oil in a large saucepan, add the onions and cook, covered, for 25-30 minutes until they're soft and golden, stirring them from time to time to prevent them from sticking. Stir in the garlic and cook for 2-3 minutes longer before adding the stock. Bring to a boil and let the soup simmer, uncovered, for 10-15 minutes. Season with salt and pepper and a dash of fresh lemon juice. Serve into individual bowls and put the cheese on top.
SERVES 4-6

BROCCOLI AND RED BELL PEPPER SOUP

You can use purple sprouting broccoli, or the larger pieces of broccoli, for this cheering winter soup.

2 Tbs butter
1 onion, peeled and
  chopped
1 pound broccoli
1 small red bell pepper

2-3 Tbs cream
  (optional)
salt and freshly ground
  black pepper

Melt the butter in a large saucepan, put in the onion, cover and cook for 5 minutes. Separate the broccoli florets from the stems, chop both and reserve a cupful of the florets. Put the rest of the broccoli, stems and florets, into the saucepan with the onion, cover and cook for a further 5 minutes, then add 2½ cups of water or vegetable stock. Bring to a boil, cover and simmer for about 15 minutes, or until the broccoli is very tender.

Meanwhile, in another pan, bring 1¼ cups of water to a boil and cook the remaining florets for just a few minutes, until they are tender. Drain the liquid into the soup, put the florets into a colander and refresh under cold water so that they keep their bright color. Also prepare the red bell pepper. Cut it into quarters and put these, shiny-side up, on a broiler pan. Broil them for 10-15 minutes, until the skin has blistered all over and begun to char, turning them as necessary. Remove from the broiler, cover them with a plate to keep in the steam, and leave until they're cool enough to handle. Slip off the skins with a sharp knife – they'll come off easily – and rinse the bell peppers. Cut into dice.

When the soup is done, whizz it to a smooth purée in a food processor or blender and return it to the pan. Adjust the consistency at this stage – add a little more water or some milk if it needs thinning, also the cream, if you're using it, along with the cooked florets and salt and freshly ground black pepper to taste.

Serve the soup in warmed bowls, with a spoonful of diced red bell pepper on top of each one.
SERVES 4

CREAM OF WINTER RUTABAGA SOUP WITH CINNAMON

Although you can make this soup for next to nothing, it tastes surprisingly luxurious with its velvety texture and hint of cinnamon.

2 Tbs butter
1 onion, peeled and
  chopped
½ cinnamon stick
1¼ pounds rutabaga
4 Tbs light cream

salt and freshly ground
  black pepper
caramelized onion
  rings to garnish
  (optional)

Melt the butter in a large saucepan, put in the onion, cover and cook with the cinnamon stick for 10 minutes. Peel the rutabaga and cut it into small dice, then add these to the pan. Stir, cover and cook gently for a further 5 minutes. Add 6 cups of water and bring to a boil. Simmer for about 20 minutes, or until the rutabaga is very tender.

Remove the cinnamon stick, whizz the soup to a smooth purée in a food processor, then pour it through a strainer back into the saucepan. Stir in the cream and season with salt and freshly ground black pepper. Garnish with caramelized onion rings which are made by frying onion rings in a little olive oil or olive oil and butter for 10-15 minutes, until they are brown and crisp. Drain them on paper towels and float a few on top of each bowlful of soup.
SERVES 4

Carrot can be used instead of rutabaga for a change.

WINTER VEGETABLES AND HERBS

GOLDEN ROULADE OF LENTILS WITH SAGE AND ONION FILLING

This is really an interesting variation on a lentil loaf; the mixture is baked flat, then rolled up around a tasty filling of caramelized onions and chopped sage. It's good served with some lightly cooked broccoli and roast potatoes.

Dried sage can be used instead of fresh although the color is not so good, and you'll only need 2 teaspoons.

8 ounces split red
   lentils
4 Tbs butter or
   margarine
1 pound onions,
   peeled and chopped
2 Tbs lemon juice
salt and freshly ground
   black pepper

2 Tbs chopped fresh
   sage
butter or margarine for
   basting
sprigs of fresh sage to
   garnish

Set the oven to 400°F. Put the lentils into a saucepan with 2 cups of water and bring to a boil. Reduce the heat, cover and leave to cook gently for 15-20 minutes, or until the lentils are tender, then beat in half the butter or margarine.

While the lentils are cooking, fry the onions in the remaining butter or margarine for 10-15 minutes, allowing them to brown, then remove from the heat. Add the lemon juice and salt and pepper to taste to the lentils, then spread the mixture out on a piece of parchment paper to make a rectangle 7 × 11 inches. Spread the onions evenly on top and sprinkle with the chopped sage.

Starting at one of the short ends, carefully roll up the lentil mixture, using the paper to help you. Keeping the roulade on the paper, lift it on to a cookie sheet then remove the paper. Brush the surface of the roulade generously with softened butter or margarine, then bake for about 20 minutes, basting it again after 10 minutes, until it is heated right through. It should be brown and crisp on top, but be careful not to over-cook it or it will dry out.

Carefully lift the roulade on to a plate, garnish it with a few sprigs or leaves of sage and serve at once, with the Rich Mushroom Gravy, below, or a Tomato and Red Wine Sauce (see page 94). Roast potatoes and winter vegetables such as leeks and carrots, or Brussels sprouts make an excellent accompaniment.
SERVES 6

RICH MUSHROOM GRAVY

2 Tbs olive oil
1 onion, peeled and
   chopped
1 garlic clove, crushed
1½ cups mushrooms,
   washed and chopped
2 tsp cornstarch

2-4 Tbs soy sauce
1 tsp vegetarian
   bouillon powder
½ tsp yeast extract
   (optional)
salt and freshly ground
   black pepper

Heat the oil in a medium saucepan, put in the onion and cook it, uncovered, for 5 minutes, so that it browns a bit. Add the garlic, some ground black pepper and the mushrooms, and cook for a further 5 minutes, continuing the browning process. Add 2½ cups of water and bring to a boil. Blend the cornstarch with some of the soy sauce, add some of the boiling liquid, then tip the whole lot back into the pan. Add the bouillon powder and the yeast extract, if using, then let the mixture simmer gently for about 10 minutes, to thicken and give the flavors a chance to develop. Adjust the seasoning as necessary – you may not need any salt – and serve with the roulade.

OPPOSITE: *Golden Roulade of Lentils with Rich Mushroom Gravy*

ROASTED WINTER VEGETABLES WITH HORSERADISH SAUCE

Roasting brings out the flavor of winter vegetables in a delightful way. They make an excellent accompanying vegetable, but I like to eat them on their own, as a complete course, with lemon juice squeezed over them, a good sprinkling of crunchy salt flakes and a tangy horseradish sauce. Leave out the garlic if you wish, but when it's cooked, it becomes very mild and almost creamy, and it's easy to pop the cooked garlic cloves out of their skins with a knife and fork.

12 ounces celery root	FOR THE SAUCE
12 ounces parsnips	1-2 tsp prepared
12 ounces rutabaga	horseradish
12 ounces red onions	⅔ cup sour cream or
2 Tbs butter	thick, creamy yogurt
2 Tbs olive oil	salt and freshly ground
1 head garlic	black pepper
lemon wedges	
(optional)	

Set the oven to 400°F. Put a large pan of water on the stove to heat. Peel the celery root, parsnips and rutabaga, then cut them into chunky pieces. Trim the tops of the onions and peel off the outer skin without removing the root; cut the onions into quarters, still leaving the root, which will hold them together.

Put the butter and olive oil into a roasting pan and put it into the oven to heat up; meanwhile, put the vegetables into the pan of water and boil them for 5 minutes. Drain the vegetables, put them into the sizzling hot fat and put them into the oven.

Meanwhile, break the garlic into cloves. Add the unpeeled garlic to the vegetables after about 15 minutes, then roast them for a further 15-20 minutes, or until they are golden brown. Serve at once, garnished with lemon wedges, if using, and accompanied by the sauce.

OPPOSITE: *Roasted Winter Vegetables with Horseradish Sauce*

To make the sauce, simply stir the prepared horseradish into the sour cream or yogurt and add seasoning to taste.

SERVES 2-4

VEGETABLE GOULASH

The idea behind this recipe was to make a vegetable version of a traditional goulash or, strictly speaking, paprikash (since it contains sour cream), using white root vegetables instead of white meat. It makes a warming yet light winter dish; I like it with buttered kale, and perhaps a baked potato.

2 pounds white root	½ tsp caraway seeds
vegetables: turnips,	salt and freshly ground
kohlrabi, celery root,	black pepper
parsnips	⅔ cup sour cream
8 ounces onions	
2 Tbs butter	
1 Tbs mild paprika	
pepper	

First, prepare the root vegetables by peeling them, then cutting them into even, bite-sized pieces; peel and chop the onions. Melt the butter in a large saucepan, put in the onions, cover and cook gently for 5 minutes, then add the root vegetables, paprika and caraway and stir well. Pour in a scant ½ cup of water or vegetable stock and add a teaspoonful of salt. Cover tightly and leave over a gentle heat for 45-60 minutes, or until the vegetables are very tender and bathed in a glossy brick-red sauce. Keep an eye on it and add a tablespoonful of water if it looks as if it's sticking. Stir in 2 tablespoons of sour cream, check the seasoning, then serve, with the rest of the sour cream.

SERVES 2

To make buttered kale, allow 4-8 ounces of kale for each person. Remove any tough stems, then shred the kale. Bring 1 inch of water to the boil in a large saucepan, put in the kale, cover and cook for a few minutes, until the kale is just done. Drain, add butter, salt and freshly ground black pepper.

BABY WINTER SQUASH WITH SAGE, CREAM AND GRUYERE

This is based on a recipe in The Savory Way, *by Deborah Madison. These baby squash, or 'miniature pumpkins' as Deborah Madison calls them, make an excellent, easy meal. They are particularly good with the Chicory and Orange Salad which follows.*

4 baby squash (but not the tiny miniature ones with soft skins)
salt and freshly ground black pepper
4 sage leaves
⅔ cup light cream
1 cup grated Gruyère cheese

Set the oven to 350°F.

Slice the tops off the baby squash and scoop out the seeds. Sprinkle the insides with salt and grind in some pepper. Stand the squash in a casserole, snip a sage leaf into each one, pour in a spoonful of cream and divide the cheese between them, pushing it into the cavities. Replace the squash tops. Bake the squash until they're tender, around 35-45 minutes, but don't let them overcook and burst.

Serve immediately, with the salad.

SERVES 4

CHICORY AND ORANGE SALAD

For this simple, colorful salad, wash a head of curly endive, shake it dry and put it into a bowl, tearing the leaves roughly as necessary. Then, holding them over the bowl to catch the juice, cut away the peel and pith from 4 oranges – ruby red oranges are lovely in this salad if you can get them – then slice them into thin circles and add them to the bowl.

OPPOSITE: *Baby Winter Squash with Chicory and Orange Salad*

Sprinkle in a little salt and grind in some pepper to taste. The salad can be left at this point, or you can add a tablespoonful or two of olive oil.

SPICED RICE WITH LEEKS AND RED KIDNEY BEANS

Serve this with a tomato and green bean vinaigrette.

1 cup brown Basmati rice
1 onion, peeled and sliced
½ tsp cumin seeds
¼ tsp chili powder
½ tsp turmeric
1 cinnamon stick
3 cloves
1½ pounds leeks
1¾ cups canned red kidney beans
salt and freshly ground black pepper

Wash the rice in a strainer under cold running water until the water runs clear, then put the rice into a heavy-based saucepan with the onion, cumin seeds, chili powder, turmeric, cinnamon stick, broken in half, and the cloves. Pour in 2½ cups of boiling water and put over a moderate heat. Bring back to a boil, then put on a tight-fitting lid, lower the heat and leave to cook gently for 15 minutes.

Meanwhile, remove the roots and outer leaves from the leeks, and slit them down the sides so that you can open them up and wash them under cold water. Then cut them into ½-inch lengths. After the rice has been cooking for 15 minutes, put the leeks into the pan on top – but don't stir. Cover and leave it to cook for a further 10 minutes, after which put the drained kidney beans into the pan on top of the leeks. Cover and cook for a further 5-10 minutes, until the kidney beans are hot, the leeks tender, the rice cooked and all the water absorbed.

Remove from the heat and season to taste. Fork through gently to mix everything and fluff the rice before serving.

SERVES 4

Some canned beans contain sugar, others do not. I prefer to use ones without sugar. If you would rather use dried beans, soak 1 cup overnight, drain, put into a pan with plenty of water, boil hard for 10 minutes, then leave to simmer for 1 – 1¼ hours, or until the beans are tender.

PUREE OF BUTTER BEANS WITH ROSEMARY AND BAKED ONIONS

This combination is very warming and good even though it's simplicity itself to put together. It makes a complete meal, although you could serve some steamed carrots or wilted spinach, too, for a bit of extra color and flavor. I generally use canned butter beans (lima beans) to save time – I choose the ones canned in water and salt but without sugar.

8 medium onions,
  unpeeled
3½ cups canned
  butter beans, or
  prepared dried butter
  beans
good sprig of fresh
  rosemary

coarse salt and freshly
  ground black pepper
butter
extra chopped fresh
  rosemary to garnish
olive oil

Start by preparing the onions. Wash and dry them, then place them, unpeeled, on a dry cookie sheet or in a roasting pan. Bake in a hot oven – 450°F – for 30-45 minutes, or until they feel tender when pierced with a sharp knife.

When the onions are almost done, prepare the purée. Put the butter beans into a saucepan (together with their liquid) and heat gently until they are very hot, then drain them but keep the liquid. Mash the butter beans or whizz them to a smooth purée in a food processor, adding enough of the reserved liquid to make a creamy consistency. Add the rosemary – you can whizz this with the butter beans if you're using a food processor, otherwise chop it by hand. It's best to add it a little at a time, as it's quite pungent. Season the butter bean purée with salt and pepper, then reheat it and keep it warm until you're ready.

Put two onions on each plate – you can leave them whole, or break them open – and put some butter, coarse salt and freshly ground black pepper on each, along with the purée. Just before serving, top the purée with a bit more chopped rosemary and a spoonful of good olive oil.

SERVES 4

CURRIED ROOT VEGETABLES WITH CILANTRO RAITA

Any root vegetables can be used for this warming winter dish: carrots, kohlrabi, celery root, parsnips, along with some cauliflower and spices. This is one of those dishes that is even better the next day, after the flavors have had a chance to develop thoroughly. Serve simply with the cilantro raita or, for a more substantial meal, with some cooked rice.

2 pounds mixed root
  vegetables
4 Tbs olive oil
2 onions, peeled and
  chopped
1 green chili
walnut-sized piece of
  fresh ginger root
4 garlic cloves, crushed
½ tsp turmeric
2 tsp ground coriander
2 tsp ground cumin

1¾ cups canned
  tomatoes
1 small cauliflower
salt and freshly ground
  black pepper

FOR THE RAITA
1¼ cups plain
  low-fat yogurt
3-4 Tbs chopped fresh
  cilantro leaves

Peel the root vegetables and cut them into dice. Heat the oil in a large saucepan, put in the onions, cover and cook for 10 minutes. Halve, seed and slice the chili, being careful to wash your hands afterwards and to keep the juice away from your eyes. Peel and grate the ginger, then add the chili and ginger to the onions, together with the garlic, turmeric, ground coriander and cumin. Give it a good stir, add the root vegetables and stir again. Cover and let it cook gently for a minute or two. Meanwhile, drain the juice from the tomatoes and measure it. Chop the tomatoes and add them to the pan; make up the tomato juice to 1¼ cups, and add that too. Bring it to a boil, then cover and cook for 15-20 minutes, or until the root vegetables are almost tender.

Meanwhile, cut the cauliflower into quite small pieces and add to the other vegetables in the pan; stir well, cover and cook for a further 10 minutes or so until the cauliflower is tender. Stir in salt and pepper to taste.

To make the raita, simply mix together the yogurt and chopped cilantro, stir well, then season with salt and pepper. Serve with the curry.
SERVES 4

CABBAGE TAGLIATELLE WITH CREAM CHEESE AND MUSHROOM SAUCE

In this recipe, young green cabbage is treated like tagliatelle and served with a creamy sauce, to make a delicious main course. The Tomato and Basil Vinaigrette which follows goes particularly well with it.

1 pound green cabbage	**salt and freshly ground**
1 cup small cultivated	**black pepper**
mushrooms	
1 Tbs olive oil	
⅓ cup Boursin cheese	
flavored with	
garlic and herbs	

Fill a medium-large saucepan with 2 inches of water and put on the stove to heat up. Wash the cabbage, removing the stalk and any damaged leaves, then shred it into fine, long strips, like tagliatelle. When the water boils, put in the cabbage, cover the pan, and let it cook for 4 minutes or until just done.

Meanwhile, wash and slice the mushrooms and fry them in the olive oil for 3-4 minutes, until they are tender. Drain the cabbage, put it back in the hot pan with the mushrooms, and stir in the cream cheese and a little salt and freshly ground black pepper to taste. Serve immediately.
SERVES 2

LEEKS PARMESAN

Another very simple dish which tastes really good. I like it as a quick and easy main course, but it also makes an interesting first course baked in little individual ramekins.

1 pound leeks	**½ cup grated Parmesan, freshly grated is best, but you can get away with ready-grated**

Set the oven to 400°F. Trim the roots from the leeks, then cut off any tough-looking green parts. Slit them down the side then wash them under cold running water, opening up the layers so that you get out all the sand. Cut the leeks into 1-inch lengths. Bring 2 inches of water to a boil in a medium saucepan, put in the leeks, cover, and cook for 7-10 minutes, or until they feel tender when pierced with the point of a sharp knife.

Drain the leeks – keep the liquid as it makes very good stock – and put them into a shallow ovenproof dish. Sprinkle the Parmesan cheese on top so that the leeks are covered, then bake for 20-30 minutes, until the top is golden brown and crisp. Serve at once, from the dish.
SERVES 2

TOMATO AND BASIL VINAIGRETTE

For this salad, which I shamelessly make all the year round now that firm tomatoes and fresh basil are available, simply slice 1-2 tomatoes for each person and put them into a bowl. Tear up some fresh basil leaves and add these to the bowl, along with a splash of red wine vinegar, a little olive oil and a seasoning of salt and a grinding of pepper. Mix it all together and serve.

You can also make a good vegan version of this by mixing the leeks with a knob of margarine before putting them in the dish, and by using ground almonds instead of grated Parmesan cheese for the topping.

125

WHOLE WHEAT PASTA TWISTS WITH BROCCOLI AND CREME FRAICHE

For a long time I avoided whole wheat pasta, having had some unfortunate experiences with it. However I've recently started experimenting with it again, and I've had some pleasant surprises, this dish being one of them. I find the nutty flavor of the pasta goes really well with the creamy, fresh sauce. I like to serve this with a tomato and basil salad like the one on the previous page.

8 ounces whole wheat pasta twists
1 Tbs butter
salt and freshly ground black pepper
1 pound broccoli
½ cup ricotta or cottage cheese
1 cup crème fraîche

Bring a large pan of water to a boil, then put in the pasta, bring the water back to a fast boil, and cook the pasta for about 8 minutes, or as suggested on the package, testing it just before the time given. Drain the pasta, return it to the pan and add the butter and salt and pepper to taste.

While the pasta is cooking, prepare the sauce. Bring 1 inch of water to a boil in a large pan; wash the broccoli and cut into florets, removing tough stems. Put the broccoli into the boiling water, cover and cook for about 3 minutes, or until it is just tender. Drain, then stir in the ricotta or cottage cheese, crème fraîche and salt and pepper to taste. Keep the sauce warm until the pasta is done, but don't let it get near boiling point.

Serve the pasta out on to warmed serving plates and spoon the sauce on top.
SERVES 4

SPLIT PEA AND SPINACH DHAL — WITH RAITA AND CHUTNEY

I find this a pleasant combination of flavors and colors just as it is; but for a more substantial meal you could add some fluffy cooked brown rice.

1 cup yellow split peas
1 onion, peeled and chopped
1 garlic clove, chopped
1 green chili
2 tsp cumin seeds
½ tsp turmeric
8 ounces tender spinach leaves, stalks removed
squeeze of fresh lemon juice
salt and freshly ground black pepper

FOR THE RAITA
½ cucumber
1¼ cups plain low-fat yogurt

FOR THE CHUTNEY
4 tomatoes
1 small onion, peeled and sliced
1 Tbs lemon juice
1-2 Tbs chopped fresh cilantro leaves

Put the split peas into a medium-large saucepan with the onion and 3¾ cups of water, the garlic, the whole green chili, cumin and turmeric. Bring to a boil, then let it simmer, half-covered, for about 45 minutes, or until the peas are very tender and the mixture is thick but not sticking. Put in the spinach and cook for a further few minutes, until the spinach is tender. Add the lemon juice and salt and pepper to taste.

While the dhal is cooking, prepare the accompaniments. Peel the cucumber then cut it into small dice. Put these into a bowl and stir in the yogurt and some salt and pepper. For the chutney, slice the tomatoes and put them into a bowl with the onion, lemon juice, chopped cilantro and salt and pepper. Stir, then leave on one side for the flavors to blend. Serve the raita and chutney with the dhal.

OPPOSITE: *Whole Wheat Pasta Twists with Broccoli and Crème Fraîche*

SEASONAL DESSERTS

TANGERINE SYLLABUB

You can whisk these up in no time for a refreshing end to a meal. They're rich, so serve small portions – wine glasses make ideal containers for them.

4 tangerines
⅔ cup heavy cream
1-2 Tbs sugar,
  or apricot
  no-added-sugar
  preserves to taste

TO DECORATE

curls of tangerine peel

Wash two of the tangerines, then grate the zest part of the rind finely into a bowl. Add the cream, stir, cover and leave for at least 30 minutes (or as long as overnight) for the flavors to infuse. Strain the cream through a nylon strainer into another bowl, pressing through as much of the oily rind as you can, to give flavor but to keep the texture of the syllabub smooth. Squeeze the juice from all the tangerines and add to the cream.

Half-whisk the cream, then stir in sugar or no-added-sugar apricot preserves to taste. Whisk again, fairly gently to prevent curdling, until the mixture makes soft peaks, then spoon the mixture into small individual serving bowls or glasses.

Cover and chill until ready to serve, but don't make these too far in advance as the mixture may begin to separate after about an hour. Decorate with the tangerine curls before serving.

SERVES 4

ARMAGNAC PARFAIT

This parfait is a wonderful dessert for a special occasion; as it's rich it freezes to a velvet-smooth texture without any stirring, so you can put it straight into a mold and just turn it out for serving. The better the quality of the armagnac, the better the result. It makes an excellent Christmas dessert.

6 egg yolks
⅔ cup sugar

2½ cups heavy cream
4 Tbs armagnac

Put the egg yolks into a bowl and whisk until they are pale and thick, preferably using an electric beater.

Prepare a syrup by putting the sugar into a medium saucepan with 4 tablespoons of water. Heat gently until the sugar has melted, then let it bubble for a minute or so until a drop of it on the back of the spoon forms a thread when pulled with a teaspoon. (It reaches this stage very quickly.) Immediately remove the pan from the heat and pour the syrup on to the egg yolks while you whisk them. Continue to whisk for 4-5 minutes, until the mixture is cool and very thick and creamy.

Whip the cream until it holds its shape, then fold it into the egg yolk mixture, along with the armagnac. Pour the mixture into a suitable container and freeze until firm. Remove from the freezer about 15 minutes before you want to serve the parfait, and serve in scoops.

SERVES 6

OPPOSITE: *Tangerine Syllabub*

RICH CHOCOLATE ICE CREAM

This is very rich and smooth. It's my favorite chocolate ice cream recipe, and one of my all-time favorite chocolate dishes.

5 Tbs unsweetened cocoa powder	7 ounces bittersweet chocolate, at least
4 egg yolks	50% cocoa solids
¾ cup sugar	
5 cups light cream	

Put the cocoa into a bowl with the egg yolks and sugar and blend to a smooth paste with some of the light cream. Put the rest of the cream into a saucepan and add the chocolate, broken into pieces. Heat the cream and chocolate over a gentle heat until the chocolate has melted and the mixture just comes to a boil. Pour some of it over the cocoa mixture, mix well, and pour the cocoa mixture back into the saucepan. Heat gently, stirring frequently, until the mixture thickens enough to coat the back of the spoon, but don't let it boil. (This only takes a minute or so.) Take it off the heat and let it cool, stirring from time to time to prevent a skin from forming.

Pour the cool mixture into a plastic container and freeze until it is solid around the edges. Then beat it well and put it back into the freezer until solid. Remove it from the freezer 15 minutes or so before you want to eat it, to give it a chance to soften up a bit.

SERVES 8

CRANBERRY AND CINNAMON CHEESECAKE

6 ounces graham crackers	⅓ cup sugar
6 Tbs butter	1 Tbs lemon juice
1 tsp ground cinnamon	½ tsp real vanilla extract
⅞ cup Philadelphia cream cheese	
2 cups sour cream	FOR THE TOPPING
1 egg and 1 egg yolk	½ cup cranberries
	⅓ cup sugar

Set the oven to 325°F.

Put the graham crackers on a chopping board and crush them to crumbs with a rolling pin. Melt the butter in a medium saucepan, then mix in the cracker crumbs and cinnamon. Spread the mixture evenly over the base of an 8-inch springform cake pan and press it down with a jar. Put this into the oven for 10 minutes while you make the filling.

Put the cream cheese into a bowl and beat until it is smooth, then gradually beat in the sour cream, egg and egg yolk, sugar, lemon juice and vanilla, to make a smooth, fairly liquid mixture. Pour this into the pan on top of the crumb base and bake for 1-1¼ hours, or until the cheesecake is set, and a wooden toothpick inserted into the center comes out clean. Turn off the oven but leave the cheesecake in there for 1 hour, then cool and, finally, chill it. The cheesecake benefits from several hours of chilling, or overnight.

To make the topping, wash the cranberries and remove any damaged ones. Put them into a saucepan with 1 tablespoon of water and cook gently for about 5 minutes, or until the cranberries are tender but not mushy. Add the sugar and heat gently until the sugar has dissolved. Boil for 1-2 minutes, until the mixture looks quite jammy, then remove from the heat and pour evenly over the top of the cheesecake.

SERVES 6-8

For a lemon and star fruit variation of this cheesecake, omit the cinnamon. Add a good teaspoonful of grated lemon rind to the cheese mixture. Instead of cranberries, spread ⅔ cup of soured cream over the top of the cheesecake after it is cooked, then leave it in the oven for 1 hour to cool down, as described. Decorate with star fruit, cut thinly to produce pretty stars.

OPPOSITE: *Cranberry and Cinnamon Cheesecake*

WINTER MENUS

MENU

A CHRISTMAS DINNER FOR SIX

Watercress and Red Bell Peppers with
Mascarpone

Christmas Wreath with Cranberries
and Porcini Sauce
Carrots in Parsley Butter
Baby Brussels Sprouts
Cock's Comb Roast Potatoes
Christmas Salad with Truffle Oil

Armagnac Parfait (see page 128)

COUNTDOWN

Up to a week before:
Make the Armagnac Parfait.

The day before:
Make the Porcini Sauce and the Vinaigrette for the
salad. Prepare the Christmas Wreath ready for baking;
prepare the carrots, sprouts and potatoes, ready for
cooking. Broil and peel the bell peppers; wash the
watercress and the salad vegetables and store in
plastic bags in the fridge.

1½ hours before:
Set the oven to 325°F. Parboil the potatoes, heat oil in
the oven, and put the potatoes on to cook; put the
Christmas Wreath into the oven about 1 hour before
the meal. Assemble the Watercress Appetizer; make
the Christmas Salad but don't toss it.

10 minutes before:
Prepare pans for the carrots and sprouts; gently reheat
the sauce. Cook the sprouts and carrots just
before you sit down to the meal; drain them, put into
warmed serving dishes and keep warm.

WATERCRESS AND RED BELL PEPPERS WITH MASCARPONE

The colors in this dish make it look like Christmas-on-a-plate! If you prepare the bell peppers in advance, have the watercress washed and the dressing already made in a jar, the dish can be assembled in moments.

2 large red bell peppers
bunch of watercress
  (about 3 cups)
6 Tbs olive oil
2 Tbs wine vinegar

salt and freshly ground
  black pepper
1 cup mascarpone
  cheese

First prepare the bell peppers. Cut them into quarters, then put them shiny-side up on a broiler pan and broil at full heat until the skin has blistered and begun to char. Move them halfway through the broiling so that all the skin gets done. Leave until they're cool enough to handle, then slip off the skins with a sharp knife and rinse the bell peppers under cold water to remove the seeds. Cut the bell peppers into long thin strips, put them into a shallow container, cover and keep cool.

Wash and remove stems from the watercress as necessary; put into a plastic bag in the bottom of the fridge until required. Make a quick vinaigrette by putting the oil into a jar with the vinegar, some salt and a grinding of pepper; shake well, then keep until required.

To assemble the dish, put some sprigs of watercress on six small plates and arrange some red bell pepper on top, dividing it among the plates. Then, using two teaspoons, put heaped teaspoons of mascarpone dotted around on top, about five to a plate. Coarsely grind some black pepper over the mascarpone. Give the vinaigrette a quick shake, then spoon a little over each plate.

OPPOSITE: *A Christmas Dinner for Six*

CHRISTMAS WREATH WITH CRANBERRIES

A dramatic centerpiece for a Christmas meal, this Christmas wreath goes well with all the traditional trimmings, and slices well both hot and cold. I love the strong taste of Stilton, but Cheddar, goat cheese or even feta could be used for different flavors, according to your taste; and you can replace the broccoli with celery root or other vegetables.

To accompany this menu, choose either a medium - or full-bodied red such as Côtes du Rhône (domaine bottled), Claret or Chianti Classico ; or a medium - dry, fruity white such as Bouches-du-Rhône.

1½ pounds large leeks
1½ pounds broccoli
butter for greasing
  the mold
9 ounces Stilton
  cheese, grated
⅔ cup light cream
4 eggs, beaten
3 Tbs chopped fresh
  parsley
6 tsp chopped fresh
  thyme

salt and freshly ground
  black pepper

FOR THE CRANBERRIES
1 cup cranberries
2 Tbs cherry and red
  currant sugar-free
  preserves
sprigs of flat-leaf
  parsley and rosemary
sugar to taste

Trim the leeks and remove any tough leaves. Slit the sides of the leeks and rinse them thoroughly under cold running water, then cook the leeks in a large saucepan of boiling water for about 20 minutes, or until they are very tender. Drain well – the water makes good stock for the sauce – refresh the leeks under cold water, and drain well again. Trim any tough stems from the broccoli, then chop it into fairly small pieces. (There should be 6 cups after trimming.) Cook the broccoli for about 5 minutes in boiling water until tender, then drain.

Set the oven to 325°F. Grease a 6-cup ring mold generously with butter. Lay single leaves of leek down the sides and base of the ring, going right round until it is all covered. Let the ends hang over the edge for the moment, don't cut them. Chop the rest of the leeks finely and mix with the cooked broccoli, Stilton cheese, light cream, eggs, parsley, thyme and salt and pepper to taste. Pour the mixture into the mold – it won't quite fill it, to allow the mixture to rise a little during cooking – and fold the overhanging leek leaves over the top. Put the ring into a baking pan and pour boiling water around, to come about halfway up the mold. Cover with aluminum foil and bake for 1 hour, or until the mold is set.

While the mold is cooking, prepare the cranberries for the decoration and sauce. Wash the cranberries, removing any bad ones. Reserve some for decoration, and put the remainder into a saucepan with the sugar-free preserves. Cook gently for about 5 minutes, or until the berries are soft but not mushy. Remove from the heat.

When the mold is done, take it out of the oven and remove the foil. Loosen the edges of the mold, then turn it out on to a large round warm plate. If a small amount of liquid appears in the center, blot it up with paper towels.

Arrange leaves of flat-leaf parsley and a few tiny sprigs of rosemary all round the top, to resemble a Christmas wreath, then arrange a few cranberries on top, at intervals, to resemble holly berries. Add a few cranberries and sprigs of rosemary around the base if you wish. Sweeten the rest of the cranberry mixture to taste as necessary, and serve it in a bowl or jug, to accompany the wreath.

PORCINI SAUCE

The wine makes this extra rich and tasty, but it is also extremely good without it – simply increase the amount of stock instead.

¾ ounce (about ¾ cup)
  dried porcini
2 cups vegetable stock
4 Tbs butter
1¼ cups dry red or
  white wine

1 Tbs Madeira wine or
  brandy
1 Tbs heavy cream
salt and freshly ground
  black pepper

Put the porcini into a saucepan with the stock and bring to a boil; remove from the heat and leave them to soak for at least 1 hour, or even overnight. After this, strain the stock into a bowl through a very fine strainer or a piece of cheesecloth. Chop the porcini finely, by hand or in a food processor.

Melt the butter in a medium saucepan and add the porcini; cook over a gentle heat for 5 minutes, then add the liquid you drained off the porcini, along with the wine. Bring to a boil, and let the mixture bubble away for several minutes until it is reduced by half. Stir in the Madeira or brandy and the cream, and season with salt and freshly ground black pepper. Serve with the Christmas Wreath.

CARROTS IN PARSLEY BUTTER

You can use baby carrots, or larger ones cut into matchsticks, allowing 1½ pounds for six people. Scrape and cut the carrots as necessary – baby ones will just need washing – then cook them in boiling water to cover for 4-5 minutes, or until they are just tender. Drain, add a knob of butter, 1-2 tablespoons chopped parsley, a squeeze of lemon juice and salt and freshly ground black pepper to taste.

COCK'S COMB ROAST POTATOES

Choose about 2 pounds of even-sized potatoes and scrub them. Put them into a saucepan, cover with water and parboil for 5 minutes or until they are reasonably tender. With a sharp knife, remove the skins and cut the potatoes in half widthways. Standing each potato on its cut surface in a baking pan, cut slits in the top, about ¼ inch apart.

Melt 4 Tbs butter, brush this all over the potatoes then sprinkle them with salt. Bake these with the Christmas Wreath, putting them at the top of the oven and allowing 1-1¼ hours for them to become golden and crisp.

BABY BRUSSELS SPROUTS

If you can get really tiny Brussels sprouts, they can be cooked whole; otherwise, with larger ones, I prefer to cut them in half as I find they do not go soggy this way. Either way, you'll need 1½ pounds for six people. Trim the sprouts as necessary, then cook in ½ inch of fast-boiling water, with a lid on the pan, for 3-5 minutes, or until they're just done. Drain, add a little butter and some salt, freshly ground black pepper and grated nutmeg.

CHRISTMAS SALAD WITH TRUFFLE OIL

Some truffle oil (which you can buy at specialist delicatessens) makes this salad extra special. Choose tender salad leaves – ordinary lettuce, plus some field lettuce (mâche) makes a good combination, or a good continental salad bowl mix. Have the leaves washed and ready, stored in a plastic bag in the fridge. Make up a vinaigrette by putting 3 tablespoons truffle oil into a jar with 1 tablespoon red wine vinegar, some salt and a grinding of pepper; shake well, then keep until required.

Just before you want to eat the salad, give the dressing a quick shake, then pour it into a salad bowl; put in the leaves on top of the dressing, toss the salad gently, and serve.

MENU

A WINTER BUFFET FOR TEN TO TWELVE

A Trio of Dips - Roquefort, Goat Cheese and
Fresh Herb

❧

Celery Root Terrine with Red Bell Pepper Sauce
Warm Red Cabbage and Cherry Tomato Salad
Broccoli and Brie Bake
Lettuce and Watercress Salad

❧

Compôte of Exotic Fruits
Fruits Dipped in Chocolate
Chocolate Truffles

❧

Mulled Wine

— COUNTDOWN —

The day before:
Prepare and bake the Celery Root Terrine; make the
Red Bell Pepper Sauce. Prepare the Broccoli and Brie
Bake ready for baking, cover well. Make
the Chocolate Truffles and the Exotic Fruit Salad.

Several hours before:
Make the dips; cover and keep in a cool place. Make
the Red Cabbage Salad but don't add the tomatoes.
Wash the lettuce and watercress, keep in a
plastic bag in the fridge; make the
dressing. Prepare the Fruits Dipped in Chocolate.

10 minutes before:
Preheat the oven; 20-30 minutes before you
want to eat, put in the Broccoli Bake. Make
the Mulled Wine. Finish making the
Red Cabbage Salad and the Lettuce Salad.

ROQUEFORT, GOAT CHEESE AND FRESH HERB DIPS

These dips are all simple to make and, I think, particularly good with some crudités, although potato chips and tortilla chips are popular with them too.

FOR THE ROQUEFORT DIP

½ cup Roquefort
cheese or similar blue
cheese
½ cup ricotta cheese

FOR THE GOAT CHEESE DIP

½ cup fairly firm goat
cheese
½ cup ricotta cheese
a little milk or sour
cream

FOR THE FRESH HERB DIP

1¼ cups sour cream
3-4 Tbs chopped fresh
herbs: chives,
marjoram, chervil, for
instance, as available
salt and freshly ground
black pepper

Either whizz the Roquefort and ricotta cheese to a cream in a food processor, or crumble the Roquefort into a bowl then mash with a fork, gradually adding the ricotta until the mixture is smooth and creamy.

Make the goat cheese dip in the same way; a food processor is probably best if the goat cheese has a rind on it; or you could cut this off, depending on its state. If the dip seems a little dry when the ingredients have been mixed together, add a little milk or a little of the sour cream that you've got for the next dip, to soften it.

To make the fresh herb dip, put the sour cream into a bowl then stir in the chopped fresh herbs and some salt and freshly ground black pepper to taste.

OPPOSITE: *Dishes from A Winter Buffet for Ten to Twelve*

CELERY ROOT TERRINE WITH RED BELL PEPPER SAUCE

This is an excellent terrine which slices well either hot or cold and goes well with many fall or winter vegetables.

As an alternative to – or as well as – the mulled wine, I'd suggest serving a light dry white wine such as Muscadet.

1½ pounds celery root	FOR THE RED BELL
2 Tbs butter	PEPPER SAUCE
1 cup grated Cheddar cheese	2 Tbs olive oil
⅓ cup freshly grated Parmesan cheese	2 onions, peeled and sliced
4 Tbs snipped chives	2 red bell peppers
3 eggs	⅔ cup stock
salt and freshly ground black pepper	salt and freshly ground black pepper
cherry tomatoes and chives to garnish	1 Tbs cold butter

Other root vegetables such as carrots or parsnips could be used to make the terrine as a change from celery root.

Set the oven to 325°F. Line a small loaf pan with a piece of parchment paper to cover the base and extend up the short sides; grease the other sides. Peel the celery root, cut it into even-sized chunks and cook in boiling water to cover for about 15 minutes, or until tender. Drain – the water makes wonderful stock – then add the butter and mash, but don't purée because some texture is good in this dish. Mix in the Cheddar and Parmesan cheeses, the chives, eggs and salt and pepper to taste.

Spoon the mixture into the prepared pan and level the top. Bake for about 50 minutes, or until the terrine feels firm to the touch, looks golden brown and a wooden toothpick inserted into the middle comes out clean.

While the terrine is baking, make the red bell pepper sauce. Heat the oil in a saucepan, put in the onions and cook with a lid on the pan for 5 minutes. Meanwhile, wash the bell peppers and cut them into rough pieces – there's no need to remove the seeds because the sauce will be strained. Add the bell peppers to the onions and cook gently, covered, for a further 5 minutes. Pour in the stock, cover and simmer for about 10 minutes, or until the bell peppers are tender. Purée the sauce in a blender, strain into a saucepan and season to taste.

When the terrine is cooked, remove from the oven and slip a knife around the sides to loosen, then turn it out on to a warmed plate. Garnish with halved cherry tomatoes and small strips of chives. Just before serving, bring the sauce to a boil, remove from the heat and whisk in the butter, a little at a time, to make the sauce glossy. Serve with the terrine.

WARM RED CABBAGE AND CHERRY TOMATO SALAD

Halfway between a cooked vegetable dish and a salad, this goes well with many winter dishes.

1 pound red cabbage	4 Tbs snipped chives
1 onion	salt and freshly ground black pepper
2 Tbs olive oil	
2 Tbs red wine vinegar	
8-12 ounces ripe but firm cherry tomatoes, halved	

Wash and shred the cabbage as finely as you can; peel and slice the onion. Heat the oil in a large saucepan and put in the cabbage and onion, cover and cook gently for about 10 minutes, or until the cabbage is tender, stirring from time to time; finally, add the vinegar. This can be done in advance.

Just before you want to serve the salad, gently re-heat the cabbage; stir in the cherry tomatoes and chives, check the seasoning and serve.

BROCCOLI AND BRIE BAKE

Although the flavor and texture of real Parmesan cheese cut from a block is best for many dishes, for this particular one, I prefer to use ready-grated Parmesan cheese from a carton. It makes a particularly dry, crunchy, golden-brown topping which contrasts well with the creamy sauce formed by the Brie melting into the cream in this dish.

1½ pounds broccoli	**¾ cup ready-grated**
12 ounces Brie	**Parmesan cheese**
⅔ cup light cream	

Set the oven to 400°F.

Wash the broccoli and cut the florets into smallish pieces. Pare the stems with a sharp knife or a vegetable parer to remove the tough, outer layer, then cut the stems, too, into small pieces. Cook the broccoli in 1 inch of boiling water, or in a steamer, for 4-5 minutes or a bit longer, until it is just tender. Put the stems in first and give them a minute or two before adding the florets, which cook more quickly. Drain the broccoli and put it into a shallow casserole.

Cut up the Brie, including the rind, and add it to the casserole, distributing it evenly. Pour over the light cream. Mash the broccoli and the Brie into the cream a little with a fork, then sprinkle the Parmesan over the top, to cover it evenly. Bake for 15-20 minutes, or until the surface is bubbly, golden-brown and crisp.

LETTUCE AND WATERCRESS SALAD

Two Boston lettuces and a bunch of watercress will be ample for this buffet. Have the lettuce and watercress washed and ready, stored in a plastic bag in the fridge. Make up a vinaigrette by putting 3 tablespoons olive oil into a jar with 1 tablespoon red wine vinegar, some salt and a grinding of pepper; shake well, then keep until required.

Just before you want to eat the salad, give the dressing a quick shake, then pour it into a salad bowl; tear the leaves roughly and put them in on top, toss the salad gently, and serve.

COMPOTE OF EXOTIC FRUITS

Lichee nuts make a fragrant base for this dish. You can use canned lichees but rinse off the syrup before using them. To these I've added papayas, which are sweet and excellent as long as they're ripe – they should be flecked with yellow and give a little when lightly pressed. Persimmons are ripe when they feel quite soft to the touch. Together, these fruits make a compôte which is sweet but refreshing and needs absolutely no accompaniment.

1½ pounds lichee nuts	**4 ripe persimmons**
2 large ripe papayas	

Remove the hard skin and pits from the lichee nuts; put the flesh into a bowl. Cut the papayas in half, scoop out the shiny black seeds, remove the peel and cut the flesh into pieces. Add to the bowl. Quarter the persimmons, cut off the skin and slice the quarters into pieces; put into the bowl with the rest of the fruit. Give it a stir, then cover and leave for an hour or so, or until required.

The flavors will blend and the juices will run, making a little natural syrup; if you leave it overnight in the fridge, this syrup will become almost jellied.

FRUITS DIPPED IN CHOCOLATE

Choose a selection of fruits for this, according to taste; grapes, strawberries and cape gooseberries are particularly good. You can use all dark chocolate, or a mixture of dark and white.

8 ounces bittersweet chocolate, at least 50% cocoa solids	*about 1½ pounds assorted fruits*

Break the chocolate into a bowl set over a pan of simmering water and heat gently until it has melted. Wash the fruits and dry them carefully, then dip them into the chocolate so that they are half-coated. Put them on a rack covered with parchment paper and leave to set.

CHOCOLATE TRUFFLES

These are a bit fiddly to make, but they are a really special treat. This quantity makes about 30 truffles.

8 ounces bittersweet chocolate, at least 50% cocoa solids, broken up	*unsweetened cocoa powder, confectioners' sugar, finely chopped toasted hazelnuts to coat*
1¼ cups heavy cream	

Put the chocolate and cream into a bowl set over a saucepan of simmering water and heat gently until the chocolate has melted. Remove from the heat and cool quickly by placing the bowl in a bowl of cold water. Once it is cold and beginning to set, whisk it hard until it's thick and light – an electric beater is best for this. (If it refuses to go thick, it isn't cold enough yet. Put the bowl back in cold water

OPPOSITE: *Sweets from A Winter Buffet for Ten to Twelve*

and leave for a few minutes longer.) Put the whipped chocolate mixture into the fridge to chill until it's solid enough to shape.

Sprinkle a tablespoonful of cocoa on to a plate then, using two teaspoons, put generous teaspoonfuls of the chocolate mixture on top of the cocoa. Sift another tablespoonful of cocoa on top, dust your hands with more cocoa, then quickly roll the teaspoonfuls of mixture between your palms to make truffles, adding more cocoa to coat as necessary. Repeat the process using the other coatings in the same way. Put them on to a small plate and chill until needed.

MULLED WINE

Popular with almost everyone, mulled wine makes a very cheering drink with which to welcome your friends on a chilly winter's night.

2 oranges	*2 glasses Cointreau or*
12 cloves	*other orange liqueur*
1 cinnamon stick	*(about ¼ -½ cup)*
2 bottles red wine	*a little sugar to taste*

Scrub the oranges, stick the cloves into them, cut them into slices and put them into a stainless steel or enamel saucepan with the cinnamon stick, wine and liqueur. Heat gently to just below boiling point, then keep at this temperature for 10-15 minutes. Taste and add a little sugar as necesssary. Ladle into warmed glasses and serve while still warm.

❧ INDEX OF RECIPES ❧